DATE DUE

MY 19 '95			
DE 22 '95			
AP 5 '96			
DE 2 '97			
FE 18 '99			
DE 1 '02			

DEMCO 38-296

Controversy.

Offensive slurs are found scrawled on a dormitory bulletin board. A stream of racist jokes is broadcast on a student radio station. Stories of a "new racism" crop up in newspapers across the nation. But do the headlines fit the reality? Is there really a new spirit of racial intolerance on campus? And if so, what—or who—is its source?

To find out, John H. Bunzel conducted extensive surveys and one-on-one interviews of students at one of America's most highly regarded institutions of higher education. In *Race Relations on Campus: Stanford Students Speak*, Bunzel—a former university president and member of the U.S. Commission on Civil Rights, now at the Stanford University–based Hoover Institution—relates the surprising and enlightening tale those students tell.

JOHN H. BUNZEL

RACE RELATIONS ON CAMPUS
STANFORD STUDENTS SPEAK

**The
Portable Stanford
Book Series**

**Published by the
Stanford Alumni Association**

THE PORTABLE STANFORD is a book series
sponsored by the Stanford Alumni Association.
The series is designed to bring the widest possible
sampling of Stanford's intellectual resources into the
homes of alumni. It includes books based on current
research as well as books that deal with philosophical
issues, which by their nature reflect to a greater degree
the personal views of their authors.

THE PORTABLE STANFORD BOOK SERIES
Stanford Alumni Association
Bowman Alumni House
Stanford, California 94305-4005

Library of Congress Catalog Card
Number: 91-067818
ISBN: 0-916318-49-4

**To
Philip Siegelman**

For friendship as it was meant to be

About the Author

A enior research fellow at the Stanford University–affiliated Hoover Institution since 1978, John H. Bunzel has a long history as an educator, writer, and political commentator.

After spending three years in the Army during World War II, the Manhattan-born Bunzel majored in political science at Princeton. Upon graduation in 1948, he proceeded to earn his master's degree in sociology at Columbia the following year and his doctorate in political science at the University of California–Berkeley in 1954.

Dr. Bunzel taught at San Francisco State University from 1953 until 1956, when he joined Michigan State University's political science department. Two years later he came west again—this time to Stanford, where he stayed for six years. He left in 1963 to return to San Francisco State, serving as chairman of that school's department of political science from 1966 to 1969. In 1970, Dr. Bunzel was appointed president of San Jose State University, where he remained until 1978.

Dr. Bunzel's experience extends beyond teaching and administration. He is the author of numerous books, including *The American Small Businessman* (Knopf, 1962); *Anti-Politics in America* (Knopf, 1967); *Challenge to American Schools: The Case for Standards and Values* (Oxford, 1985); and *Political Passages: Journeys of Change through Two Decades, 1968–1988* (Free Press, 1988). He has written over one hundred articles for such publications as the *Washington Post, New York Times, Wall Street Journal, Los Angeles Times,* and *The Public Interest.*

Dr. Bunzel, a past president of the Northern California Political Science Association, was a California delegate to the turbulent 1968 Democratic National Convention. In January 1974, the San Francisco Board of Supervisors honored him with an award for his "unswerving devotion to the highest ideals of brotherhood and service to mankind and dedicated efforts looking to the elimination of racial and religious bigotry and discrimination." In 1983, President Ronald Reagan appointed him a Commissioner of the U.S. Commission on Civil Rights, a position he held until 1986. During the election years 1984 and 1988, he delivered weekly political commentaries for CBS Radio in San Francisco. In 1990, he received the Hubert Humphrey Award from the Policy Studies Organization for years of service as "an outstanding public policy practitioner."

An avid amateur scholar of the role of humor in American society, Dr. Bunzel plays golf, relishes Chinese food, and loves all kinds of music.

Editor-in-chief: Della van Heyst
Series Editor and Manager: Bruce Goldman
Book Design/Production Manager: Amy Pilkington
Cover Illustration and Design: Paul Carstensen

Table of Contents

Prefatory Note:

The Student Factor

I f we are indeed in the midst of a resurgence of racism on our campuses—which is the single recurring theme of most media accounts—then there is a pressing need for the kind of investigation and analysis that will contribute to a deeper understanding of a difficult and complex problem. In this study, therefore, I have employed the skills and techniques of what I choose to call academic journalism to inquire into the nature of black-white relations at Stanford.

The engine of the research was a series of in-depth interviews (each lasting up to 1½ hours) with 54 undergraduate students conducted during the course of the 1988–89 academic year. Of those interviewed, 20 were white and 24 were black. A number of these students lived in the Afro-American theme house, Ujamaa [See Appendix]. The focus was on black/white issues because these are the ones that are most often at the heart of the controversy not only at Stanford but on most campuses today. I was not interested in an ideological study. That, it seemed to me, would be unproductive because it would elicit only ideological responses. It would be much more useful and informative, I felt, to encourage students to talk not simply about abstract theories and ideas but about the extent to which they had experienced concrete examples of racist incidents and behavior and, if they had, to explain in their own words how it affected their lives.

I must note (with considerable amusement) that Stanford University's Panel on Human Subjects in Behavioral Sciences Research, which must give official approval to every research study undertaken on campus, was so concerned about the possibility of students becoming "anxious" or demonstrating "negative" feelings during the personal interviews that it required a "consent" statement to be read to each of them before any questions were asked. It was even suggested at one point that I consider informing the respondents that if they became too agitated or disturbed during the interview, they could call the Cowell Student Health Center for counseling and psychological services. I objected, on the grounds that this would lead students to believe—even before the conversations began—that they were about to be subjected to such mental stress that they could not escape with their emotional selves intact. I assured the Panel that each student would be told the interviews were voluntary, and that anyone who chose to participate would not be identified by name because no names would be sought. Furthermore, all responses would be kept confidential. At the conclusion of the interviews, I was able to report that there had not been a single incident of student anxiety or discomfort such as the Panel had been worried about. Not only did the students cooperate willingly and fully, but a great many of them were eager to continue expressing their views well beyond the time that had been originally scheduled.

In addition to the personal interviews, a nine-page questionnaire was mailed to a random sample of Stanford seniors—specifically, half of the senior class of 1989. The size of the sample was very large—much larger than one would need statistically—but the decision was made in light of the kinds of issues that were raised (that is, controversial and, because of the nature of the general subject, sometimes sensitive). Thus I decided on 50 percent of the senior class, selecting 862 students on a random basis. Furthermore, I was also concerned about proper black representation. Knowing that the absolute numbers were small, I went out of my way to get black respondents, identifying them through a variety of means and "over-sampling" them. The statistical rate of return was good, with the proportions of ethnic groups roughly corresponding to the racial composition of the campus as a whole. Other source material used in the study included a report of the [Stanford] University Committee on Minority Issues, informal group interviews with students, and an eight-week investigation of an incident in the Afro-American theme house that caused campus-wide debate for months.

The questions used in the senior survey (mailed questionnaire) were an outgrowth and continuation of the one-on-one questions (much less structured and more informal) that were asked of students in the personal interviews. In fact, some of those conversations proved to be so fruitful that they were incorporated into the mailed questionnaire. The difference, of course, was that the personal interviews—because they were intended to be more probing—drew out a great many more observations and opinions as well as examples of individual experiences on which these students could offer comment and interpretation. The advantage of the senior-class questionnaire is that it afforded another group of students an opportunity to offer their views, although more briefly.

Various studies show that most whites believe that color

distinctions have no place in an integrated and egalitarian society. At the same time, racists continue to spread their poison. This is what has been called "the interplay between the two halves of white America's split personality." The purpose of this study was to gain some insight into a fundamental question: Is racism today "new" and different?—different, for example, from the racism that was filtered through a 1960s American civil-rights framework; and to see if it manifests itself in different forms on the campus of a major university, and if so, how and why.

I wish to acknowledge not only the energetic work but the commitment of my research assistant, Jordan Seng, a Stanford senior when this study was undertaken, who conducted the personal interviews and provided other invaluable assistance. He represents the best of the coming generation of teachers and scholars (he is now pursuing a Ph.D. at the University of Chicago). I am also indebted to Jeanne J. Fleming, who has a Ph.D. in sociology from Stanford and who served as my research assistant on other projects in years past. Now president of Flanders Associates, a social-science research firm in Palo Alto, California, she drew the sample of the survey of the senior class and coded the results. As always, I am grateful for her professionalism and friendship.

I also wish to thank the Alexis de Tocqueville Institution for its support. I am especially grateful to John Raisian, Director of Stanford's Hoover Institution, for his interest and assistance. My appreciation, too, to Ida Lee, for her secretarial help. And I owe special thanks to Carolyn Schneck, who put her considerable talents to work in reading and editing the final manuscript.

J.H.B.

◀ **1** ▶

Overview

n the academic year 1988–89, racism was the most discussed issue at Stanford University. But Stanford was not alone—far from it. Charges of racism on American college campuses have received national attention since the mid-1980s, with virtually every semester bringing another example: a street brawl between black and white students, the occupation of a president's office, whites wearing Ronald Reagan masks and carrying a gun beating and taunting a black activist, a black dean resigning in anger. Offensive name-calling and abusive slurs—"KKK", "jigaboo", "Kill all niggers"—have been found scrawled on washroom walls and dormitory bulletin boards at some schools. At one university a stream of racist jokes was broadcast on the student radio station.

"Racism 101," a Public Broadcasting Service "Frontline" segment that aired in May 1988, began: "There are disturbing signs [that blacks on campus] face the same racial tension that plagued their parents." The increasing pace of racist acts for several years, followed more recently by fresh incidents and controversies seeming to arise almost daily, led the *Los Angeles Times* to proclaim "A New Bigotry Ripples Across U.S. Campuses." Whether sparked by the movement to oppose the concept of Western culture as inherently infected with racial prejudices, or by events as different as allegations that a respected history professor's lecture was "racially insensitive" and an interracial date at a large public university, issues of race and racism clearly have become matters of deep concern to higher education.

Yet as the stories of campus racism have developed in the media, there is disagreement not only over questions of fact but about what interpretation should be placed on many of the incidents that have been reported. Administrators, faculty members, and students are by no means united in believing that our colleges and universities are truly "racist" or that racial unrest and conflict represent an ominous trend that is causing serious injury to minority and white students alike. Most thoughtful observers acknowledge that the "redneck" racism of fights, slurs, property damage, and other acts of "ethnoviolence" does not describe the character or atmosphere of campus life today. Such ugly incidents of racial conflict have occurred—and will occur in the future—too often to be dismissed as unimportant. "But it isn't beatings or outright intimidation or things like that," said a black sophomore on a predominantly white campus. "It's feeling isolated, or being treated coolly and often condescendingly." A black student at another university said, "You feel like an Earth man visiting Mars."

This "new racism" has been described in many different ways.

Some believe the conflict between whites and blacks on campus is due more to ignorance and innocence than to deliberate bias or racial hostility. They see the campus as a community in which young people are brought together in relatively close quarters, in marked contrast to the larger society, where the degree of personal interaction with people from other groups with different backgrounds is much more limited. This can lead to egregious incidents—but it can also be more subtle, as the Anti-Defamation League's Jeffrey Ross has observed, creating "an environment of insensitivity." After all, says Ross, 18- and 19-year-olds are not known for being sensitive to intergroup situations. One black senior said that what he saw most of the time was a misunderstanding of another culture or race, leading to a lot of miscommunication—"as simple as that," he remarked.* Stephen Balch, Executive Director of the National Association of Scholars, believes it is a mistake to lump racial hostility and mere insensitivity together, as if their causes were the same. Does it really help, he asks, to label insensitivity as a form of racism, as if those who are insensitive are of a type with Bull Connor?

Others, however, see another kind of racism altogether, which they insist is neither subtle nor difficult to identify. It is an active racism—in the words of a Black Student Union leader at Stanford, it is "institutionalized racism, which is the action of your standard power structure in the university that is able to actualize prejudice and oppress others." Such observers point to actions that perpetuate "the overt and covert racism permeating our institutions," from the voting down by the faculty of proposals to require all students to take a course in ethnic studies before they graduate, the small number of black and other minority faculty members, and the unwillingness of university officials to adopt tough

---

* This and all other quoted comments by Stanford students are drawn from surveys and interviews as explained in Prefatory Note to this book, except where otherwise specified.

penalties for students who use racial slurs and epithets to harass "students of color," to the long history of "not just racist education, but the education of racists" in courses in Western culture or civilization.

Racial tensions are as much a result of perceptions as of reality. Many white students, for example, believe that blacks now have equal access to a college education, that colleges and universities are routinely developing programs and funds to support their increased and continuing enrollment, and that dramatic progress has been made in providing racial equality in society at large. Frequently questioning the validity of black students' concerns, they think blacks with lower grades and test scores today enjoy unfair advantages resulting from the preferential treatment they receive in admissions practices.

These white students see themselves as innocent victims of affirmative action policies intended to correct past discrimination. On the other hand, many black students resent the frequent assumption that they were only admitted to college because of special admissions programs. They look around and see that little has happened in terms of their numbers on campus, notes Nathan Glazer, a Harvard Professor of sociology and education. This becomes a powerful incentive for them to establish their own identity, sometimes to be more "black," sometimes more mainstream. Black students virtually all agree that white students have no understanding of the very different experience and culture they come from. Many white students, however, feel that blacks do not give them enough credit for the significant changes that have been made in race relations. "They feel a lot has been done," says Glazer. "Indifference, I would guess, is the dominant orientation of white students. Whether the term is 'indifference' or 'enough is enough,' I don't know."

No single theory or generalization can explain what has been called the "new climate of conflict" between whites and blacks in our colleges and universities today. The Reagan presidency is regularly denounced by the civil-rights community for eight years of hostility to blacks and other minority groups as well as for its rhetoric against affirmative action, school busing, and other programs aimed at helping minorities. In addition to "fostering a reactionary mentality" among many white students, the Reagan Administration is blamed for sending a signal to the nation and to college students in particular that "things done on behalf of minorities are somehow wrong." Other critics cite the pervasive perception that minorities are getting more than their share of scholarship funds and other limited resources, the increasing competitiveness of admissions at the nation's most selective schools at a time when the institutions are stepping up their efforts to recruit black and Hispanic students (thereby promoting the suspicion of favoritism among white students), the intensified competition for good jobs and affordable housing among college graduates, and the "nascent fear" among whites of the growing proportion of minorities in the U.S. population.

But the problem of racism on campus is so full of difficulties and complications as to defy agreement about either its causes or solutions. For example, while attention has been focused on racially offensive and often violent incidents, the particular conditions that give rise to them have been overlooked.

Consider the case of a large stretch of graffiti that appears on a campus building. It is immediately considered an incident. But if there is an accumulation of small graffiti in a public place— a bathroom, a library, or a dormitory—it just grows and gathers over the years. Is that an incident? Is it an incident every time somebody scrawls graffiti? Or does it simply become a condition? Universities frequently face problems of fraternity hazing. Are those incidents, or are they indicative of larger campus conditions? Jeffrey Ross of the Anti-Defamation League has said that to concentrate on the incidents themselves is to see them as aberrations rather than as part and parcel of an ongoing culture. "I think to a certain degree what we have had is a massive pothole on campus," he told the U.S. Commission on Civil Rights in May 1989. "Potholes are a phenomenon which one day you don't see and the next day you come out and there is a big hole in the ground. The question is, what happened yesterday to create the hole in the ground? But the hole in the ground wasn't created yesterday," Ross says. "It only appeared today. What you have had for years and years is subsurface erosion. I think that is really what we have been seeing on our campuses."

Many academic leaders, however, argue that racial and ethnic incidents occur on campus because of an increase in hate violence nationally—in short, that a campus merely reflects what is happening in the larger society. In this view, a college is not an ivory tower. Students have already been socialized into American society and bring onto the campus the very attitudes they have been exposed to. Yet what are those attitudes? Would anyone claim they are predominantly attitudes associated with either the old racism of segregation and discrimination or the more recent racial ugliness and violence of Howard Beach (New York)? Or are they attitudes that make it possible for an important story, seldom told in the press, to be understood for what it has become: a civil-rights success story of how *well* the majority of blacks and whites get along on campus?

Although there is no consensus on what has brought about the racial tension in our colleges and universities today, there is considerable agreement that many of the incidents of intergroup conflict on campus have emerged only since the civil-rights revolution of the mid-1960s, building on and frequently in reaction to the many gains in race relations that have been made in the last quarter century. And, in one of those twists of irony, these incidents have occurred in the very places where the civil-rights movement has had its greatest impact.

The gifted black writer Shelby Steele, professor of English at San Jose State University, believes that campus racism is a problem that misrepresents itself. It has the superficial look of America's timeless racial conflict—white racism and black protest. Part of our concern over it, he writes, "comes from the fact that it has the feel of a relapse, of an illness gone and come again." But if the symptoms are the same, Steele notes, the illness is not. The socio-political and psychological factors that drive the new racial tension today have grown out of equality more than inequality. "Campus racism," writes Steele, "is born of the rub between racial difference and a setting, the campus itself, devoted to interaction and equality." On our campuses—concentrated micro-societies with considerable interaction and adult-level competition—everything that remains unresolved between blacks and whites, "all the old wounds and shames that have been addressed, present themselves for attention—and present our youth with pressures they cannot always handle." Many of the incidents arise, Steele adds, when students protect themselves from racial anxiety, which is manifested as "guilt in white students and as feelings of inferiority in black students."[1]

Inevitably, a familiar question arises: Are there more cases of racial bigotry and hostility today, or are we just finding them because we are looking for them? While there is no definitive answer, the most reasonable answer is both. Instances of racial and ethnic conflict have steadily increased, in part because more attention is focused on them not only by the press—after all, the press has always been quick to report other (and sometimes related) pathologies such as drug or alcohol abuse or vandalism on campus—but by university administrators and faculty who are now trying to confront the problem. And there is still another reason. In the last ten years or so, many black students who feel they have been subjected to overt or subliminal pressures of racism, or that whites have been largely indifferent to their existence, are raising the heat by speaking out in louder and angrier voices. In addition to looking upon their college education as the primary credential for success in American society, they also see the campus as an arena where they can make demands for changes in admissions policies, minority faculty hiring, the structure of the curriculum, and so forth, all of which play an important role in bringing attention to their presence and in strengthening both their self-esteem and their group identity.

It is not surprising that the issue of black-white relations at Stanford has evoked a wide range of opinion and emotion from students of all backgrounds who live on campus amidst a complex set of problems and concerns. Among the top universities in the nation, Stanford is relatively young, yet its history has been one of fast and constant change. Its students are the best and the brightest that the country has to offer, a very select group of talented young people who do not have to worry about getting a job or making it in the world.

It has often been suggested that it is precisely because they have more time for intellectual discussion and argument that Stanford and other "elite" institutions are more likely to become polarized. Such generalizations, of course, only go so far. But what can be said about Stanford students—and perhaps about college students everywhere—is that they live in a world of potential and time-bound intensity, constantly discovering new capabilities and powers. As a result, they often see their university years as a time to change the campus environment as they also change themselves. As one Stanford student explained, "I expected racism to be a major issue at Stanford not because of anything I knew about the school, but just because you sort of identify the struggle against racism with the college experience."

◀ 2 ▶

Stanford and Its Students

Make no mistake about it: Stanford is a West Coast school, and the students like it that way. They study in the sun, make trips to the beach, and find things to do in Stanford's famous foothills. Healthy and athletic, they love sports, especially their varsity teams. In the spring, when there is water in the campus's Lake Lagunita, some of the favorite classes are physical-education courses in sailing and windsurfing. And don't look for the collegiate look at Stanford. To dress for success is to wear jeans and sweatshirts in the winter, baggy shorts and comfortable T-shirts in the summer. That goes for both men and women.

At Stanford, there is no peer pressure to be monastic in one's study habits. The students are conscientious about their academic work, but the key is to work without sweat, earn good grades, and enjoy the good life as well. This is not the kind of devil-may-care irresponsibility that smacks of self-satisfaction and arrogance, but simply a general reluctance to feel pressured, or at the very least to place a high value on appearing relaxed. A popular expectation among students is that one should be happy.

The campus is warm and airy. The sandstone architecture is the finest in Spanish Colonial and Western ranch. From the very beginning, when Senator and Mrs. Leland Stanford founded the University in 1885, a priority was put on open space, and much care is taken in tending to the large lawns and spacious athletic fields and championship golf course. Alumni fondly refer to the University as The Farm (it covers over 8,000 acres of land). Very simply, Stanford is a likeable place, and its students very likeable people.

The 465 students who attended Stanford on opening day in 1891 did not come from prosperous families. Because the Stanfords were eager to keep costs down so that other than well-to-do youngsters might have a chance to go to college, no tuition was charged. As a result, the new University attracted a large number of students from poorer families. When Stanford opened, in fact, half the student body was working to pay for food and lodging.

Criteria for admission closely resembled those of the nearby University of California. Students were expected to have completed high school, passed a sufficient number of qualifying examinations, or to have proof of special competence in a particular field of study. For the first ten years, until pressure from the growing number of applicants led to a more careful selection of students, it was slightly easier to be admitted to Stanford than to the state university.

By the second year, there were 764 students at Stanford, 286 of whom had come from outside of California. They represented 39 states, as well as the District of Columbia and fourteen foreign nations. Most came because of the climate, adventure, and academic freedom, and only a few for reasons of economy. In any case, the special receptivity of the University to the poor and disadvantaged was rather short-lived. By 1900 the cost of room, board, and other expenses had reached $300 for the average student, and by 1906 only 25 percent of the student body was working at one job or another. In the Twenties, Stanford began to charge tuition, which today is among the highest in the country. While Stanford maintains an admissions policy that is blind to financial need and places a special priority on recruiting minority students, the largest percentage of its students come from affluent suburbs (only 29 percent in the senior survey said they came from a city). While precise figures are not easy to come by, 70 percent of the white students and 40 percent of the black students from the set of one-on-one interviews have family incomes of over $50,000. Almost one-third of the white students come from families making over $100,000. And while nationally 47 percent of freshmen reported working six or more hours per week, only about 23 percent of Stanford freshmen did.

By any standard, the students who go to Stanford make up an elite clientele. The primary criterion for admission is distinguished academic achievement and potential, and the quality of the applicants and admitted students is very high. In 1990, for example, 45 percent of the admitted freshman class had combined SAT scores of 1400 and above; 88 percent had combined SAT scores of 1200 and above. Nationally, just 1 percent of high-school seniors scored over 1400 on the SAT, and only 9.8 percent scored above 1200. Of the admitted class, 47 percent had GPAs of 4.0, 90 percent had GPAs of 3.6 and above, and 92 percent were in the top 10th of their high-school class. In addition, data from the senior survey show that 70 percent of the mothers and 79 percent of the fathers of Stanford students have college degrees, and an impressive 57 percent of students' fathers have either a master's degree or Ph.D.

When Stanford opened its doors in 1891, women and men were both welcomed to the University. In 1899, however, Mrs. Stanford decreed that no more than 500 women could be enrolled at any one time, a cap that remained in effect until 1933, when the Board of Trustees emended Mrs. Stanford's dictum so that more women could be admitted. Women were still not given equal opportunity with men for admission, but their numbers increased. The next major change did not occur until the early 1970s, when the Faculty Senate urged the Trustees to remove limitations on the proportions of men and women and to eliminate pre-set targets for the ratio of men to women in the freshman class (but did not recommend a goal of a 50-50 ratio). Today, the gender ratio still favors men, but much less so than in the past. In the most recent freshmen classes, the ratio of men to women has held at 55 percent to 45 percent.

Since the turbulent Sixties, the Berkeley campus of the University of California has been synonymous with liberal student politics. But in surveys of incoming freshmen at UC-Berkeley and Stanford in 1988, the Stanford class was more liberal than Berkeley's. Only 15 percent of the Stanford seniors surveyed regarded themselves as even somewhat conservative. Fifty-five percent of white students consider themselves liberal, as do 89 percent of the blacks. In the presidential election of 1988, 72 percent of the Stanford students who voted cast their ballot for liberal Democrat Michael Dukakis. It is no secret that colleges generally have a liberalizing effect on their students—seniors, for example, tend to be more liberal than they were as freshmen. However, only about one-fourth of all students nationally identify themselves as liberals. If not almost unique, Stanford is remarkable in the degree of uniformity in the political outlook of its students. Most of them are liberal on social issues—according to one study, about 80 percent of the 1989 freshman class favor legalized abortion

(65 percent nationwide do), and only 13 percent at Stanford condemned homosexual relations, compared to 33 percent nationwide—and also support aggressive government solutions for the socio-economic problems of our society. Furthermore, many students increasingly are coming to respect the influences of ethnicity on different social groups, and most of them value the diverse interests and backgrounds they encounter on the campus and agree that the university curriculum, to greater and lesser degrees, should provide students with more knowledge of comparative ethnic cultures.

Before entering Stanford, most of the students have had very little contact with other groups and races. According to the school's University Committee on Minority Issues (UCMI), only 26 percent of white students say they had "quite a bit" or "a great deal" of exposure to blacks, while a majority (41 percent) had "little" or "none." As might be expected, blacks had a higher rate of exposure to whites. Especially illuminating, however, is the number of black students who come from black communities and high schools. Fifty percent of those interviewed came from a neighborhood that is mainly black, and about 45 percent came from high schools with a minority enrollment of 50 percent of more. The significance of these figures is mostly a matter of individual perceptions of the "culture shock" among blacks in a white society. One can speculate that perhaps for roughly half of the black students, living and studying at Stanford is a very new and, indeed, radical experience. The UCMI maintains that "inexperience with people from other races and ethnic groups is responsible for much of the tension between minority and white students. Even for the most well-meaning students, this inexperience often results in ignorance, misunderstanding and insensitivity, leading to social distance between individuals and groups."

The acceleration in the early 1970s in the enrollment of women was considerably different from the shift to admitting a greater percentage of minority students. For one thing, the move to bring more black, Chicano, and Native American students to Stanford was directly related to student protest on campus. The general climate of the time, of course, was already pushing the University in that direction, but the catalyst for change in admissions policy came from minority students themselves. Furthermore, the major issues that the University was grappling with in trying to respond to the students' demands (and later to those of the government) were in large part moral and philosophical: What is the University's obligation toward disadvantaged groups in general and minorities in particular? What is its responsibility to maintain its reputation and role as one of the nation's premier institutions of higher learning? Certainly Stanford was not the only university that would struggle for a long time with the problem of how to successfully integrate into its community students who were academically unprepared and culturally different.

By contrast, student pressure did not play a major role in the decision to admit more women to Stanford. There were no mass rallies and impassioned demands for justice. The discussion within the University about admitting more women was considerably more pragmatic and resigned than the debate that took place over affirmative action for minorities. For example, the financial cost to Stanford appears to have been rationally and openly assessed (the issue was raised more timidly and privately regarding minorities), as was the impact an influx of women might play in moving the University away from the engineering/science niche it had carved out for itself. Nor was there any soul-searching about either the harm done to women in discriminating against them in the past or about how more women might seriously undermine the University's "mission."

The most obvious difference, however, was that admitting more women required Stanford to evaluate only one characteristic of applicants in a new light—their gender, while admitting more minority students involved a consideration and evaluation of *all* of the characteristics traditionally taken into account in a new light. High-school grade-point averages, SAT scores, various indicators of non-academic achievement—all were thrown into question as legitimate measures of preparation and, especially, of talent and promise. And this reevaluation of what kinds of qualities students "should" have immediately opened up the larger question of what a university ought to be like. In short, class and other distinctions between most of the Stanford community and its new minority admittees posed very different (and much more profound) problems from those encountered in increasing the number of women students.

The assassination of Martin Luther King Jr. in 1968 and the outcry in the black community that followed proved to be a watershed for Stanford's policy on minority recruitment and admissions. Only days after Dr. King's murder, in a scenario repeated on campuses across the United States, representatives of the Black Student Union convened a mass meeting and presented a list of demands for immediate change to then-provost (and later president) Richard Lyman. They asked for (among other things) representation of minority groups in the student body in proportion to their numbers in the population as a whole, and for a central role to be given to black students and black faculty in evaluating minority applicants for admission.

While the Black Student Union's demand for affirmative action clearly catapulted the University into action, only months earlier the massive Study of Education at Stanford (SES) had also concluded that minority students were underrepresented on campus. Recommending that remedial action be taken at once, the SES proposed an admissions formula that gave considerably less weight to traditional academic criteria such as College Boards and high-school grade-point averages, thus ensuring that more minority students would be accepted at Stanford. Never actually put into operation, the plan nonetheless provided a guideline and legitimacy for subsequent efforts to establish new admissions criteria.

Affirmative action represented dramatic change in University policy regarding minority students, but the idea of giving some categories of applicants for undergraduate admission to Stanford an edge in the completion was not new. Like most colleges and universities, Stanford must keep a number of constituencies happy and loyal. In particular, alumni and faculty often want their children to go to Stanford, and Stanford—with a stake in encouraging generous alumni and avoiding disgruntled faculty—accords these sons and daughters preferential treatment in admissions. Moreover, other groups not defined by academic talent or track record are also given an edge—athletes and children of the wealthy or of very prominent people, to mention a few.

The first problem that Stanford (and other highly selective institutions) faced in granting special preference in admissions to underrepresented minorities was that of identifying a pool of minority high-school students who would be interested in attending the University and who could succeed if admitted. For a number of years in the 1960s, Stanford solicited the names of talented black high-school students from the National Merit Scholarship rosters. However, this pool was by no means large enough to generate the increase in numbers the University was now aiming for, particularly since other institutions were also stepping up their minority-recruitment efforts. In the 1980s, the number of minority college-bound seniors minimally eligible for admission to Stanford (or to an Ivy League school or first-rate public institution) was still dishearteningly low. High-school grade-point averages and SAT scores of Asians and whites have consistently been much higher than those of American Indians, blacks, and Hispanics. Furthermore, these three affirmative-action groups are less likely to apply to college in the first place, and less likely to have been in a college-preparatory or "academic" track in high school.

Other national data are equally sobering. In the mid-1980s, for example, fewer than 4,200 black college-bound seniors had grade-point averages of 3.75 or better. SAT scores, for all of their shortcomings, help to control for variations in high-school quality and students' course selections. Yet, out of a total of 71,137 black secondary-school seniors who registered for the Admissions Testing Program, only 66 black students had verbal SAT scores over 699, and 205 had math scores over 699. Fewer than a thousand black students had verbal SAT scores of 600 or better, and fewer than 1,700 had comparable math SAT scores.

This has posed a serious problem for first-rank institutions trying to recruit minorities. The number of well-qualified blacks and Hispanics is exhausted quickly, and the not-so-elite schools are soon left drawing from a pool that is substantially less qualified. The handful of excellent minority students simply cannot meet the numerical demand for them. The problem is not only that Stanford and other "elite" schools monopolize the very best black applicants, but that even these schools have affirmative-action goals they cannot meet with the applicants at hand. As many observers have pointed out, the best schools reach down to the next students in line—in the words of policy analyst Charles Murray, "students who would not have gotten into these schools if they were not black, who otherwise would have been showing up in the classrooms of the nation's less glamorous colleges and universities."

During the last two decades, colleges and universities throughout the country have adopted affirmative-action programs that have sought to remedy "inequity" in admissions by providing some kind of substantial representation for minority groups. The issue is no longer whether there will be affirmative action, but how much is desirable and for what purposes. At Stanford, the question of how, and how many, minority students should be admitted brought with it—as it did on other campuses— discussion and controversy over how the admissions office went about its job. On what grounds should the University give preferential treatment to minority-group members who are less qualified academically than other applicants, in order to bring about some kind of group proportionality? Acknowledging the need to have more minority students, how does the admissions office decide how many more of which minorities are needed to achieve the "right" student mix? Inasmuch as the differences in academic performance of various ethnic groups are frequently large, what is Stanford prepared to give up in academic excellence so that more members of these groups will be admitted?

Consider the question of diversity, which is central to Stanford's admissions process. Admissions officials will go only so far in their public comments about it. It is not unusual to be told that in selecting a freshman class, a key goal is "diversity," though not solely in terms of academic qualities such as grades and test scores. Thus, offers of admission to the freshman class entering in fall 1990 were sent to applicants from all states and more than forty foreign countries. California has the highest representation in the admitted class (35.5 percent), followed by Texas (6.0 percent), New York (5.8 percent), Illinois (4.0 percent) and Washington (3.9 percent). Officials also talk about "leadership potential," "character," and other "qualitative" measures that are part of the admissions formula for enriching the range and diversity of the student body. They will admit that "special sensitivity" is shown to certain ethnic-minority groups, and that membership in such a minority group is an important factor in allowing a candidate to be chosen over others who have better academic credentials. But these same officials are reluctant to discuss if or when "special sensitivity" becomes outright preference, or how far they have to "stretch" to get the representation of minorities they want. As Harvard economist Robert Klitgaard notes in his authoritative book, *Choosing Elites,* admissions officers are "conspicuously vague about their policies of preferential admissions." They prefer to point to the "diversity" they are creating.

Yet "diversity" is open to different meanings and interpretations. Is ethnic diversity desirable because it benefits society, or because it is fair and therefore good for society at large, or because it is mandated, or popular, or what? To what extent does "diversity" today refer less to the diversity of society and more to the "political mobilization" and pressures of various groups on the admissions office? How is the goal of ethnic diversity to be balanced against other factors? And can "diversity" also mask some of the criteria admissions officers use in making their decisions? When asked why Asian-American admission rates tended to be so low in the 1970s and early 1980s, university officials most commonly responded that their goal is to achieve "ethnic diversity" in their student bodies and that Asian-Americans are an "overrepresented minority." But increasing the number of students whose ethnicity is unlike that of the majority would, by definition, increase the ethnic "diversity" of the students. Besides, limiting Asian-American admissions in the name of "diversity" inaccurately assumes the homogeneity of Asian-Americans. Furthermore, the concept of "overrepresentation" is faulty when it is uniquely applied to Asian-Americans. One could only imagine the outcry if Stanford or any college or university decided to reduce its Jewish student population down to the 3 percent that Jews represent in the national population. Indeed, an argument for limiting admissions to reflect the national population levels only reinforces the idea that there exists an unwritten quota for Asian-Americans.[1]

The admissions office at Stanford today appears to evaluate and admit students by using pretty much the same criteria, both quantitative and qualitative, as in the past, but in addition earmarks minority applications for special and independent consideration. All students—minority and non-minority—submit the same application materials, and all students are evaluated on the basis of a recalculated high-school grade-point average, the rigor of the courses they took in high school, the recommendations of teachers, and the students' own "brag" sheets. Applications generally have been sorted into one of five academic ranks:

Rank 1:   High-school GPA of 3.9–4.0, top 3 percent of the class, SAT greater than 675 each, and 700+ on an Achievement test

Rank 2:   GPA 3.8+, top 5 percent of the class, SATs greater than or equal to 650 each

Rank 3:   GPA 3.7+, top 10 percent of the class, SATs greater than or equal to 600 each

Rank 4:   GPA 3.6+, top 20 percent of the class, SATs greater than or equal to 600 each

Rank 5:   Less than Rank 4

Minority applicants are not distributed among these ranks in the same pattern as non-minority applicants. Fred Hargadon, Stanford's dean of admissions from 1969 to 1984, identified three principal groups of minority applicants to Stanford: talented, successful students who would do very well; marginally well-qualified students who could survive at Stanford without remedial work but would be in the bottom quarter of their class; and students who would require considerable remedial effort to make it through four years at Stanford. Hargadon noted that the last category of students made up a significant proportion of minority admittees inasmuch as many colleges and universities are competing for better-qualified applicants. Over the years the percentage of highly qualified minority applicants has increased, but is still relatively low.

The "working bottom limit" for admission to Stanford, according to Hargadon, was "what we think is the ability to do the work here, based on preparation and the kinds of courses taken, and on the students' ability to express themselves from what we see in their applications." With this in mind, he characterized the academic "floor" for minority admittees as being in the top 20 percent of their high-school graduating class, having SAT scores totaling no less than 900, and a high-school grade-point average of 3.5 or more. Minority students who exceed this floor typically gain admission. However, the factors that go into evaluating students are not easily captured in a formula—there is no hard and fast line above which applicants are admitted. Of the black applicant pool, roughly 35 percent are offered admission, while the percentage for Hispanics is about 40 percent. It is closer to 18 percent for the total applicant pool.

The Admissions Office is extremely selective about the students it admits to Stanford, almost routinely turning away class valedictorians and applicants with a 4.0 grade-point average. The standards for evaluating minority students differ from those applied to majority students. Thus minority students are much less likely to enter in the top two academic ranks than are majority students, nor are their verbal SAT scores or high-school grade-point averages as high. In 1978, the last year such figures were available, 4 percent of minority students were in the two highest ranks and 55 percent in the lowest (Rank 5), compared to 35 percent and 12 percent, respectively, for majority students. Data that would reveal if the gap has widened or narrowed have not been made public. What is known, however, is that in the last 25 years the number of minority students at Stanford, which was about 2.8 percent of the freshman class in 1968, has increased substantially. Richard Lyman's promise to the Black Student Union in April 1968 to double the number of black students within a year (the 1967 figure was 37 black freshmen) seems to have been the last time that a numerical goal was explicitly formulated. While he was admissions dean, Fred Hargadon described his goal for affirmative action as admitting "a significant fraction, a critical mass" of minority students each year, enough in number so that they would not feel uncomfortable and so that Stanford would look attractive to prospective minority applicants. There is no evidence that formal quotas figured in his policy, nor does it appear that they do so today. Blacks, Hispanics, and Native Americans (but not Asian-Americans) are given special consideration in the admissions process. If admissions were race-neutral, Hargadon has confirmed, perhaps only one-third of the minority students would still get in.

Clearly, Stanford looks very different from the way it did in the 1960s. The entering class of 1990 was the most ethnically diverse of any freshman class in the University's history: 43 percent were black, Hispanic, Asian-American, and American Indian. Hispanic-American students made up 10.0 percent (up from 8.4 percent in 1989); Native Americans 1.1 percent (the same as in 1989); Asian-Americans 23.9 percent (up from 19.0 percent in 1989), and African-Americans 8.0 percent of the admitted class (down from 9.8 percent in 1989). The decline in the percentage of admitted black students was a reflection of the decline in black applications, not only at Stanford but nationwide—"an issue of concern to all in higher education," commented Jean Fetter, the school's dean of undergraduate admissions from 1984 to 1991. (Four percent of the admitted students were foreign, the same as in 1989; 44 percent were women, the same as in 1989.) [2]

The last ten years have also brought about other major changes. The increase in minority students has resulted in a variety of minority-student organizations and ethnic-centered programs. The Black Student Union (BSU), born in the tempestuous year of 1968, wasted little time in agitating for minority rights on campus. By the early 1970s, when the big surge in minority enrollment began, the Mexican American Student Organization, the Stanford American Indian Organization, and the Asian Students Coordinating Committee were already in place and active. The BSU petitioned for greater efforts in minority enrollment, more black faculty members, ethnic-studies courses, and an Afro-American dormitory, which ultimately became the first of several ethnic "theme houses" on campus.* In 1987, the Rainbow Agenda was formed as a multiracial organization demanding more changes in behalf of minorities. In the aftermath of several racial incidents in the residences that produced an explosion of feelings, the Rainbow Agenda was reorganized into the Students of Color Coalition, which began operation with protests and a "Mandate for Change," a list of nine demands directed at the University administration and President Donald Kennedy. The Council of Presidents (of the student body) issued a statement of full support and called for immediate action by Kennedy.[3]

Stanford has been a leader among American universities in the development of a racially diverse campus. In a relatively short period of time, it has moved well beyond the tokenism of the past when there were only a handful of minority-group members on an all-white campus. Today, for example, black students no longer feel the effects of being a rarity, of being solo individuals who are noticed and watched and tested in virtually every situation in which they find themselves. Fred Hargadon's notion of a "critical mass" may not have been precisely stated, but among its defining characteristics is a sufficient presence of other black (as well as other minority) students to effectively create a base of support and socialization that can make their interactions with the rest of the student community more comfortable.

But there is a great irony. While the increased numbers of minority students have generated a new era of race relations at Stanford, there have been more, not fewer, racial problems. Although students are regularly being told by University officials

---

* See Appendix, "Ethnic Theme Houses at Stanford."

of the importance of such concepts as "pluralism," "multicultural-ism," and "appreciation of differences"—as the UCMI reports, "incoming students now hear these themes articulated during freshman orientation and repeatedly through their undergraduate years"—the dynamics of the critical mass have led to an accumulation of underlying tensions and racial incidents, as well as frequent disagreements between white and minority students about whether the interracial environment that has emerged on campus is friendly or hostile.

◀ 3 ▶

The Beethoven Incident

O n September 28, 1988, approximately eight students, including a black junior we will call Ralph, were discussing issues of black lineage in the intersection of two hallways in downstairs Ujamaa, the Afro-American resident theme house on Stanford's campus. It was an informal conversation, and no one was particularly surprised when two white freshmen, Phil and Paul (not their real names) walked by and joined in. Phil, a Ujamaa resident, became fully involved in the discussion and challenged a young woman when she maintained that she had a pure black ancestry. This added some emotion to the interaction. Eventually, the talk turned to music, and then to the ethnic heritage of the great composers. The main issue was the lineage of Beethoven, who, some assert, may have had African ancestors. The conversation grew more intense, and at one point Ralph made a statement to the effect that all music has black origins.

That evening, Phil and Paul drank heavily. Later, in an intoxicated state, they altered a caricature of Beethoven on a poster by drawing in Negro features, including larger lips and an "Afro" hairstyle. They hung the defaced poster on the chalkboard next to Ralph's doorway; he discovered it the following morning. News of the incident soon began to spread. The Ujamaa staff planned to question all those who had participated in the discussion about Beethoven's lineage in order to identify the culprits, but no investigation took place in the next two weeks. Phil and Paul continued their usual pattern of behavior, and Phil especially was involved in several more discussions about ethnicity and black consciousness.

On Friday, October 14, a flyer advertising a black fraternity party was found in Ujamaa with the word "niggers" written across it. The reaction was immediate. An anti-white message with obscene language appeared on a chalkboard in the main Ujamaa hallway, but was quickly erased. Ujamaa staff members called a dorm-wide emergency meeting for that night.

About forty Ujamaa students attended, along with a dozen or so black students from other residences on campus. Discussion centered on the vandalized flyer, but also touched on the two-week-old Beethoven incident. Phil attended, but said nothing. Paul heard about the meeting and tried to attend, ostensibly (according to reports from some students who lived in adjacent Naranja, Paul's dorm) to apologize publicly for offending anyone. However, he arrived late and was not allowed to enter. After the meeting, an Ujamaa resident told a member of the non-official residence staff team that she had overheard a student speaking with an English accent say something about hanging a poster of Beethoven in Ujamaa. The tip led several Ujamaa upperclassmen to Paul, a Canadian with a noticeable accent, who had returned to his room. He confessed, and was taken for questioning to a meeting of Ujamaa Resident Assistants (student resident staff members) and student leaders from the Black Student Union. The questioning was heated, and a number of black students suggested that Paul should be expelled from the dormitory.

Later that evening, in the room of two resident assistants in Naranja, Paul explained that he had meant the poster to be a joke. He had gone to an elite boarding school near London where his Jewish heritage was often ridiculed, he said, and he had always laughed it off. He had expected Ralph to do the same. In fact, in the past he had commented to friends about a racially insensitive wallhanging that blacks had posted in Ujamaa. On the stairwell in the east side of the dorm, the Ujamaa staff had adorned the walls with the names of black heroes, including that of Louis Farrakhan, the black nationalist leader. Farrakhan is strongly anti-Semitic—a fact not lost on Paul, who took it as a point of discussion and debate but not as a personal offense. He had not intended the poster to be a general racist attack, he said, but a little fun-poking at Ralph. However, Ralph and the rest of Ujamaa did take offense at the defaced Beethoven poster, considering it a deliberate attack on an entire race, not a prank aimed at one individual.

The central event of the entire episode was the Sunday, October 16, meeting of Ujamaa and Naranja at which Phil and Paul made their public apology to black residents. Before the proceedings began, no one fully explained the reasons for the meeting to those who had gathered. No single person was in charge. While most of the students knew something had happened involving a racially offensive flyer, very few knew all the details. Phil and Paul stepped up to make their apology without anyone explaining their offense. All of the students and housing staff who were interviewed for this study thought, upon reflection, that many people most likely assumed Phil and Paul had hung not only the defaced Beethoven poster but the more inflammatory "niggers" flyer as well. It was the vandalized flyer that had generated the most bitter feelings in Ujamaa—the Beethoven poster, the only one which Phil and Paul confessed to hanging, had caused very little discussion for two weeks—and both freshmen reaped the emotional fallout for an offense they insisted they did not commit.

The lack of structure in the meeting provided the optimal atmosphere for the angry black students to vent their emotions without check or examination. Resident fellows at Ujamaa said later that Phil and Paul had been found "guilty by similarity of incidents." Considering the tremendous tension, it is little wonder that the meeting ended in violence. Phil and Paul's apology became only another irritant. Phil did most of the talking and, true to form, took what one student called the "intellectual approach." He explained that while he regretted the incident, he had not been intentionally malicious and did not understand the strong adverse reaction. He assured his audience that he was prepared to apologize, but that it seemed to him that Ujamaa would prefer some sort of restitution. He suggested that he and Paul present a report on the African heritage of the Russian poet Pushkin to the black cultural library in the dorm. The assembled residents interrupted him and demanded an immediate outright apology. The two freshmen—bewildered and frustrated by now, and more than a little insensitive—consented with a hollow "We're sorry." Phil's point seemed to be that he could not sincerely apologize until he understood how his offense was interpreted by black students. He asked the blacks who were present to explain their feelings to him. Several took him up on the offer, but Phil failed to engage anyone successfully in what he hoped might be a rational discussion of the issue.

A number of black Ujamaa students spoke of the injustices

they had suffered throughout their lives at the hands of racists. As they recounted their experiences, the tension in the room mounted. It became an occasion for blacks to affirm their common bonds and unity and to remind themselves of their history of subjugation. In the course of their comments, a white woman rose to ask if the fact that Phil and Paul acted while inebriated had any mediating effect on their actions. She was shouted down amidst charges of racist sympathies. As it turned out, the particular offense of Phil and Paul was never fully discussed. Accusations were leveled, but the Beethoven poster received little attention. The apology was a complete failure.

After Phil and Paul had finished their remarks, angry students wanted to know how they were to be punished. A residential dean, himself black, explained that the Office of Residential Education had decided that the problem was to be handled "in house": Phil and Paul were to remain in Ujamaa and Naranja in order to undergo an intense education in racial sensitivity by black students. The dean's solution was met with immediate disapproval. (Although several students were willing to accept the decision, they were in the clear minority.) The meeting then turned again to more personal accounts about the damage caused by racism, which injected still further emotion into an already tense atmosphere. Ralph stood up to explain his feelings about the Beethoven poster, sharing some of his experiences as a black who grew up in south Chicago and what it was like to live in such an oppressive environment. He had hoped that Stanford would be a haven from racist evils. He said he felt patronized by Phil and Paul because they had masqueraded as his friends while insulting his race behind his back. "I could kill people like you," he said, and then lunged at Paul. Several Ujamaa residents restrained him, and the room was cleared by the resident assistants. At least one black woman hyperventilated and many others sobbed. Some black residents shouted obscene, anti-white phrases at Naranja students; other blacks surrounded whites to protect them from the prospect of violence.

Phil and Paul left the dorm that afternoon and were never allowed to return. Phil immediately met with friends in Naranja and, in tears, apologized for his lack of sensitivity during the meeting. A white Ujamaa resident assistant walked around the campus with Paul, who also cried for a good part of the afternoon. By a new order from Residential Education, both of them could be expelled from the University if they were seen in Ujamaa—an order, explained the dean, given for their own protection.

The next day, flyers appeared in Ujamaa calling for the removal of all white students from the house: "NON-BLACKS LEAVE OUR HOME YOU ARE NOT WELCOME IN UJAMAA." Different anti-white flyers continued to circulate in the weeks that followed, most of them advocating a separatist dorm for blacks. Two days later an Ujamaa residential staff member discovered that someone had defaced the picture board, located in the main hallway, that displayed photographs of all the new freshmen in the house. During the night, a vandal had stuck straight pins into the faces of the pictured white students—and into the face of one black student who some considered too friendly with whites. The photo display was taken down immediately and the pictures were destroyed. Doubtless the work of a small minority of militant residents of Ujamaa, the flyers and the vandalism never reached the press and received little attention on campus. The Office of Residential Education knew about the events but made no statements. Inside the dorm, white students complained about reverse racism to the staff. One black freshman said, "After the incident, it was not a good idea to have white friends in this house."

The decision to deal with Phil and Paul "in house"—to have them "face the music" and receive some instruction in racial issues—was quickly changed. Shortly after the incident made the papers, Residential Education announced a new decision: Phil and Paul, the Office said, had violated their housing agreements, contracts that bind students "to be considerate of other residents and the residence staff; and to respect the rights of others at all times." The two offenders wound up "temporarily" housed in a guest room in another dormitory. No campus residence would take them permanently, fearing the repercussions of accepting two "convicted racists." Meanwhile, the University's judicial bodies undertook an investigation of the poster-hanging to determine whether or not they had violated the Fundamental Standard for Student Behavior, the broad code of conduct imposed on all students enrolled at Stanford. (If found in violation, they would have faced mandatory expulsion.) That the University even thought about invoking the Fundamental Standard was a function of the insistent public demands by black students for punishment of the offenders. The call for prosecution touched off a big campus debate over the merits of the Standard and what many claimed was an urgent need for a more explicit code of student behavior that would lead to immediate punishment for "racist offenses."

As it turned out, Phil and Paul did not face charges of violating the Fundamental Standard. The Dean of Students observed that the administration "didn't have all the answers" needed to fix conclusively or authoritatively the kind of punishment for students involved in cases of bigotry. "We acknowledge that we are not dealing with it effectively," he said. As a direct result of the incident, Stanford has begun an inquiry into changes in the disciplinary procedures to make them more applicable to charges of racism.

Two weeks after the incident, Residential Education offered to fund a weekend dorm trip for Ujamaa residents to a destination of their choosing as a way of helping them recover from the trauma of recent events. Although the Ujamaa residential staff was originally supportive of the idea, the outing never took place. Naranja residents generally resented the offer, viewing it as a "cave in" and a "buy off" to get Ujamaa's compliance in further anti-racism legislation. Many of the students in Ujamaa—at least initially—thought the trip was a good idea. One who did not was a black resident fellow, who said "I'm not about to drop everything and go to Disneyland just because someone else called me a nigger."

This, then, was the allegedly racist incident that took place one autumn evening on the Stanford campus. Two white freshmen had gotten drunk and hung a racially offensive poster near the door of a black student living in Ujamaa. The incident quickly escalated into a major controversy and made national headlines. Not surprisingly, the newspaper reports tended to sensationalize the issue, adding more fuel to an already open flame. A few weeks afterward someone clipped a story of the events out of a big-city newspaper and tacked it to the bulletin board in Ujamaa. The person had also taken several felt-tipped pens and highlighted every factual error in the news account. The article was awash in a rainbow of pastel ink.

One should never underestimate the power of the student newspaper to shape opinion on a college campus. The *Stanford Daily* is no exception. Its reporting of the incident was frequently selective. Many who had followed closely everything that happened in Ujamaa believed the *Daily* misrepresented events, thereby confirming the popular sentiment in many quarters that it was "pursuing a hidden agenda" or, as one student put it, "blindly supporting the liberal cause." A principal criticism was that in its first article it de-emphasized the importance of the afternoon meeting on October 16 by focusing on the retching and hyperventilating of students but failing to stress that the meeting ended in violence. It reported that students fled the meeting because of "the effects of the incidents," when, more accurately, they fled for fear of violence. Many Naranja residents overwhelmingly agreed that the *Daily* implicitly led the student body to believe that Phil and Paul had hung both racially offensive posters (a charge they consistently denied), and that the omission of particulars (e.g., the details involved in the discussion of Beethoven's ancestry) as well as the use of front-page pictures of Phil and Paul served to stigmatize the two freshmen and contributed to the unwillingness of any campus residence to take them in. Furthermore, some Naranja and Ujamaa students—minority and non-minority—criticized the *Daily* for not printing anything about the backlash of anti-white incidents, including the separatist flyers and the defacing of the pictures of white freshmen in Ujamaa.

The incident in Ujamaa became the center of intense and often inflammatory discussion throughout the academic year. The black community at Stanford worked together to protest racism on campus. What began as an immediate partnership between the Ujamaa staff team and the leadership of the Black Student Union grew into a reorganized political coalition of minorities (the Students of Color Coalition), one of whose first actions was to stage an anti-racism rally that drew widespread media attention. The homosexual community, the Jewish community, and the United Stanford Workers Union threw their support behind the alliance and its protests. The student senate passed a bill "to support demands made by students of color in response to racial incidents at Ujamaa." On October 28, Jesse Jackson came to the campus and gave the anti-racist agenda of the Coalition his personal endorsement.

The incident clearly had profound political repercussions. But, more significantly, it also had powerful ramifications for the relations among blacks and whites as tension grew in the days that followed. In Ujamaa, 96 percent of the residents interviewed two to four months after the events reported an increase in racial alienation and segregation. As Stanford's dean of student affairs observed, what happened in Ujamaa provided "a gripping case study of behaviors that were troubling to many and which occurred in a complex web of action and reaction."

Lost in the midst of it all were Phil and Paul. Virtually everyone agreed that their actions should not be minimized and that in making their apology they had displayed arrogance and insensitivity. But beyond that there was wide disagreement about the meaning and implications of the highly publicized Ujamaa incidents, including a persistent question about whether or not they were the actual source of the outcry on campus that took place afterward.

◀ **4** ▶

The Views and Experiences of Black and White Students

hen Stanford students are asked what they mean by racism, it quickly becomes clear that in a number of important respects the differences among them are pronounced. That racism is morally unacceptable is a judgment to which no one takes exception. But as it is used in conversation and discussion, the term "racism" is very much a matter of language and perception. Thus it is foolish to ask students (or anyone else) "What should be done about racism on campus?" without determining what they believe is the nature and significance of the problem—in short, without first asking, "What are we dealing with?"

When two students defaced a poster of Beethoven by giving the composer black features and an Afro and then hung the picture near the door of a black dormmate, Stanford immediately found itself added to the list of campuses where white racism was said to be on the upswing. The students who called the incident racist believed it was a personal insult tainted with negative judgments against an entire race. What became known as Stanford's "racial incident" was viewed as an act of prejudice and stereotyping, in much the same way that the discovery of a swastika painted in the basement of one of the campus dorms was protested as evidence of student racism. When the word "racism" was used in the campus debate that followed, students generally meant, as one white senior suggested, "selective prejudice, much more of an attitude than an action." One Asian senior said that racism is the "degrading or devaluing of other people because of their color." These are the definitions of racism generally given by most students—that is, irrational attitudes of hostility against individuals or groups because of their background or membership in one race or another. In the senior survey, 34 percent defined racism as prejudice, by which they meant preconceived and unfavorable judgments about people; another 32 percent cited both prejudice and discrimination ("selective mistreatment"). A significant number of students stated that implicit in their idea of racism was the belief that people of all races can be racist. As one freshman woman said, "It's prejudice against another racial group. It can work both ways, blacks against whites and whites against blacks."

By contrast, a high percentage of black students—especially in the one-on-one interviews, where they had an opportunity to express their thoughts more fully and accurately—defined racism in terms of its structural manifestations, repeatedly formulating the problem as one of "institutional racism." Half of them spoke of the oppression of one racial group by the racial group in power. Little was said about white prejudices and stereotypes;

indeed, many black students maintain outright that racial stereotypes have little to do with racism. "Racism is the action of a group in power which is able to oppress others," explained a black freshman. Other black students talked about "a systemized oppression of a certain race," "oppression of specific ethnic groups," and "a system of rule and domination on a worldly level along the lines of race."

In short, not only do more black than white students see racism at Stanford—among those interviewed, only 20 percent of the whites but 60 percent of the blacks said racism was a "very serious" issue on campus—but blacks are also much more likely than whites to regard it as the exercise of institutional authority or (in the more familiar idiom) the "white power structure" on campus. Some examples of what blacks mean by racism also came when, in the survey, graduating seniors were asked to evaluate several different situations. Over 70 percent of the blacks, as compared to fewer than half the whites, described the presence of a large number of whites among the tenured faculty as "definitely" or "probably" racist. Almost 84 percent of the black students said the Western orientation of the curriculum—because it does not have enough courses rooted in the cultures and traditions of the Third World—is racist. These situations were seen as further confirmation that racism is entrenched in the structure of the University.

Not surprisingly, the seniors' attitudes were related to their political views. Thus black students, women, and those who identify themselves as politically liberal were considerably more likely than others to believe that the white/non-white tenure ratio and the "Westernized" curriculum are racist. Blacks and liberals were more likely to believe that the low proportion of blacks receiving academic honors represents racism. Liberals were far more inclined to think that white students socializing mainly with other whites, and blacks having lower grade-point averages on the whole, are examples of racism. But perhaps more significantly, when white and black students were asked to rate situations in which whites socialize principally with whites and blacks with blacks—both of which are perceived as more interpersonal than structural—a much smaller number of black than white students characterized these socializing situations as racism.

In recent years, the demands made by black organizations on Stanford's campus have focused on issues they regard as fundamental if there is to be real change within the University—an ethnic-studies graduation requirement, the hiring of more minority faculty, the appointment of minority students to the Board of Trustees. It is through political and organizational statements, which portray racism in terms of the collective struggles for racial power, that the black student leadership (and much of the black community) at Stanford has found a voice. What is striking is that in the formal rhetoric there is little talk of interpersonal relations between blacks and whites, which was a recurrent theme in many of the speeches of Martin Luther King Jr. Dr. King constantly asserted that the aim of his movement was ultimately interpersonal, "to win the friendship of all the persons who had perpetrated this [racist] system in the past." Black student leaders today insist on basic changes in the "power relations" on campus. White students, however, are primarily concerned with interpersonal relations.

There is a special difference between those who regard racism as simple prejudice, discrimination, and stereotyping and those who define it as involving systematized behavior by the racial group in power: The former believe all groups are capable of racism, whereas in the latter view only those "who control the levers of power" can appropriately be called racist. According to this latter definition, "white racism" is redundant. Many who used this definition frequently distinguished between prejudice and racism. "Prejudice is not really racism," explained one white senior, "until you stick it into your standard power structure."

While any and all groups may use stereotypes, make prejudg–ments, and discriminate, only whites can truly be racist because only they have the power to oppress. As one black student put it, "It's the difference between being the colonizer and the colonized. If you're black, the pressure is always to be like the colonizer instead of who you are." Many who hold this view of campus racism maintain that racism is inherent in the American social and economic system, a system that was "created by whites and today is still run chiefly by whites." However, only a little over 20 percent of the black students interviewed say that Stanford is racist—and 40 percent of these students say this is so for no other reason than that the University is part of a larger racist society. Furthermore, only 12 percent of the senior class believe that Stanford is a racist institution.

It is relatively easy for students to talk about racism in more or less abstract terms. For example, half of the seniors surveyed say they have seen racism against minorities, and roughly half of all minorities say they have been the target of racism on campus.[1] However, getting students to specify concrete examples of racism based on events or incidents they have personally encountered is much more difficult. The number of those inter–viewed reporting firsthand experience with racist behavior is quite low—only 5 percent of the white students, for example, and under 30 percent of the blacks, most of whom describe the racism they ran up against as "subtle" and "hard to explain" to nonblacks. A survey conducted by Pacific Management Systems for the University Committee on Minority Issues (UCMI) concluded:

> Only a few of the minority students and none of the white students cite personal observations or experiences of overt racism on Stanford's campus. . . . the bulk of minority students report frequent acts of covert racism or devaluation they experience as "subtle, elusive, difficult to pinpoint, and insensitive" . . .

These actions have been humiliating, devaluing, or caused them to experience episodes of self-doubt or loss of confidence.

When white students discuss the racism they have seen on campus, they tend to talk of negative views and comments—usually couched in the familiar language of racial stereotypes—that reflect either prejudice or acts of discrimination:

A teacher signaled out a quiet black girl, telling her that as the sole representative of her race in the course, it was her responsibility to forget white misunderstanding, forcing the student into an uncomfortable and public position.

My friend, who normally is desperate to get a date, will turn down any black guy who asks her out, just because he's black.

A white and previously sheltered freshman was placed with a black freshman from the South Bronx and the white female was constantly criticizing the "crude ways" of her roommate. They hated each other by the end of the year.

An athletic coach referred to a national team from China as a bunch of "chinks."

I heard about an incident in a sorority on campus. The group was playing charades and a white girl guessed "nigger." The black girl in the group said nothing. The pledge trainer was black, and she didn't say or do anything. The whole incident was kept under the rug.

Some of the examples of prejudice or discrimination are directed against Jews rather than racial minorities. "I'm Jewish," says one student, "and I've experienced several anti-Semitic attacks by other students—students telling me that I should have been put in the gas chambers, insensitivity in the administration and food service to religious needs and concerns, swastikas on campus." Another student says that "a lot of it comes from inadvertent comments like 'Stop being Jewish' when someone refuses to loan money." Several respondents also reported numerous instances of students making disparaging remarks about homosexuals.

The accounts by black students of the racism they experience at Stanford are very different—and very different from the violent and malicious racism they often faced before coming to Stanford, underscoring the fact that overt racism is much less of a problem on campus than off. One black woman told the story of being the only black child on a military base, where she was beaten by other children because of the color of her skin. "I asked them why they hit me," she recounted, "and they said, 'My father says people like you need to be hit like this.'" A black freshman woman remembered being "beaten all the time for being black by the other kids. I got a pencil shoved in my eye one time. It got so bad that my parents moved me to a private school." Another black woman who was the only black student in her high school told of her struggles for social acceptance: "No one would date me because I was black. I thought I was the ugliest thing in the world." Another black student said that his parents had filed a law suit against an employer for discrimination in the workplace. Some students recalled racially motivated gang fights, and more than a few talked of battling high-school teachers who did not believe that blacks could excel in the classroom. Very simply, these students painted clear portraits of the racism that remains a problem in our country.

But Stanford, it is equally clear, is both much more and much less than a microcosm of American society. Most of the black students who said they had personally encountered racist behavior at the University (as mentioned earlier, they numbered barely more than one-fourth of those interviewed) were hard-pressed to describe what it was like or how it worked—because, as many of them said, the racism they confronted, although it pervaded the whole campus, was subtle and could not be effectively explained to others. "I've felt like an outcast in classes," a black senior woman noted. "The class breaks up into study groups and people don't want you in theirs." A black freshman said, "There's nothing that's actually been done to me, but there are things that have been hurtful—like people who don't think black writers have anything to say." Others just talked of subtle changes in the behavior of whites in the presence of a black, and a certain tension they felt in social situations. White students have repeatedly heard these complaints of subtle racism and are largely bewildered by them. As one senior put it, "It's hard to know how to react to charges of racism when there are no specific incidents or examples. That's pretty damn subtle."

If subtle racism is hard to define or analyze, "subconscious racism"—a term widely used on campus in recent years—raises all kinds of problems (and especially for the researcher). It appears that this notion of subconscious racism is a product of the exploration of the roots and symptoms of subtle racism. Roughly one-third of the white and black students who were interviewed said that personal racism might be a matter of one's subconscious, that "a person can be racist without ever fully knowing it," as one of them explained. A good many students said that negative stereotypes may be a problem of "the unconscious psyche." Yet how informatively can individuals discuss racism if they cannot be certain of their own actions? "I don't know, I might have some racist tendencies," confessed one white freshman, "but I really try to watch my step." Black students offer a limited catalog of insensitive statements or questionable actions, but seldom anything blatantly offensive. One white freshman woman could well have been speaking for many other white students when she said, "I've learned how easily comments that seem innocent to you can be misconstrued. But whether or not they are really intended to be racist—unfortunately, that seems almost irrelevant today."

A question frequently raised is whether an individual can commit an act of racism without racist motives. Yes, we are told, if the person is subconsciously racist. But how is that to be demonstrated, and by whom?

Only a small number of students who talked at length of their personal experiences with racism on campus said anything about institutional racism. Yet a rather high percentage (and blacks at a rate double that of whites) felt that institutional racism exists at Stanford. As it turns out, this is not the paradox it may at first appear to be. It is, after all, not especially strange that few students establish a logical or causal connection between themselves and institutional racism when they think of individual incidents or offenses. Racism that manifests itself in the structure of the University is a collective phenomenon and difficult to perceive on a personal level. When pressed for specific definitions, the students who answered used different words but came up with the same reply: Institutional racism is discrimination within the processes of the institution. However, only a relative few were able to cite specific examples. Of the 50 percent of blacks who agreed that institutional racism exists on campus, 22 percent could not come up with a concrete example. Of the small number of white students who said there is institutional racism at Stanford, 60 percent could not provide an example. The few who did pointed almost without exception to racial bias in the curriculum, the small number of minority faculty members, and the absence of severe punishment for those who commit "racially offensive acts."

The important point is that students are much more likely to perceive institutional racism than racism in general. Blacks, as we have indicated, are likely to think of racism as a structural phenomenon. Upwards of 90 percent of white students, however, define racism in interpersonal terms, yet only 5 percent of those interviewed said they had actually seen or experienced racism on campus. One-fourth of them believe that institutional racism exists, but only a few offered any examples.

Given the way in which the term is used by many students, it is not hard to understand why institutional racism has a conversational function similar to the role of subconscious racism. The reasoning has the qualities of a syllogism: There is evidence that racism exists in society and, to a lesser degree, on campus; most whites have had no exposure to racist behavior before coming to Stanford, and most whites and blacks say they have had no firsthand experience with racism after entering the University; still, racism must exist, and the concept of institutional racism—conveniently ambiguous—confirms the existence of racist elements without requiring anyone to accuse individual persons, groups of people, or even specific offices on campus of wrong-doing.

When students talk about racism, in a significant number of cases they talk about "reverse racism"—discrimination against whites. While no questions were asked about it directly in the one-on-one interviews, a number of white students spoke about (as one of them put it) "the sort of reverse racism that discriminates against whites in the undergraduate-admissions process, where minority applicants are granted affirmative-action preferences." In the survey of graduating seniors, approximately one out of ten cited reverse discrimination or some form of prejudice against whites. One-half of the white students interviewed reported some firsthand experience with reverse racism at Stanford, compared to only 5 percent who said they had been exposed to racism in general, and each of them had a specific illustration. In the survey conducted by UCMI, almost half of the white students said they had experienced some form of discrimination or devaluation because of their skin color. "My application [for a campus job] was denied because I was too late for the deadline," said a white senior. "But the committee was still seeking applications from 'people of color.'" Others tell of similar experiences. "Down in the dining hall," explained a white freshman, "when I go and sit at those 'black' tables, they look at me like, 'What's he doing here?'" Another student said she felt that "the BSU's attitude toward whites is a racist view itself. I feel like I've been the target of racism since I am not a person of color."

One of the most telling findings is that since coming to Stanford, 30 percent of white students have become more suspicious of the "anti-racism" of minorities. In some manner (and in varying degrees), the struggle of blacks and other minority students is alienating a large number of whites, making them less likely to pursue understanding and reconciliation with the minority communities on campus. After the incident involving racially offensive posters hung in Ujamaa, a number of students reported strong anti-white sentiment. "Some blacks distributed anti-white flyers in the dorm, " recounted one Ujamaa resident. "Because I was one of the whites who spoke my mind and challenged some of the things they were saying, I got one slipped under my door." A white freshman in Ujamaa also told of problems with the flyers:

> After the incident, some of the whites in Ujamaa who were concerned about the anti-white flyers had a meeting—I mean, we were offended by them. The Ujamaa staff asked us not to take the story about the anti-white flyers to the *Daily*, and promised us that they would make an official statement about it. They never made the statement. That offended me. It was the first time I ever had anyone attack my race. They said it was only a few people that produced the flyers, and that we had to keep it down. Well, two people doing the offensive Beethoven poster— that doesn't represent the feeling of most whites!

A white freshman woman who lived outside of Ujamaa

complained, "I feel like a lot of blacks are defensive. Some black guys in the dorm won't talk to me." Indeed, most of the examples of reverse racism were about situations in which black students were defensive, distrustful, or angry toward whites, a reaction (or so one may surmise) against the devaluation that blacks feel they suffer from white students. In any case, whites were clearly frustrated by the development.

Within the black community, there was also some of the same frustration. When asked in the personal interviews to define racism, a number of the blacks volunteered that discrimination was practiced by blacks against whites. Said one black freshman woman, "The only racism I've seen at Stanford is reverse racism. I get a lot of pressure because I'm dating a white man. The black upperclassmen don't like that." Another black woman explained, "Blacks and whites interact more on the other side of campus than they do on the [Ujamaa] side, because over there you're not being watched by other blacks. Have you ever heard the term 'miscellaneous'? It's what blacks get called when they hang out too much with whites. It's terrible. Once you get called that, you have to do something amazing to get away from it." In a world in which blacks are still confronted with racism, it is not difficult to understand a certain distrust they may feel toward whites. But it is a source of tension in campus race relations, including tension among blacks. The distrust of different races cuts both ways.

When students were asked if their ideas about racism had changed during their attendance at Stanford, 65 percent of whites and 44 percent of blacks acknowledged that their experience as undergraduates had often been a strong influence in changing the way they thought about the issue. One-fourth of the whites and a little more than a fifth of the blacks said that they had become more aware of the problem—meaning one of two things, or both. Perhaps racism on campus is so obvious that students have been rudely confronted with its complications and are therefore more sensitive to the way it works. Or it may be that because the University at all levels, including students themselves, regularly provides education about racism, the general level of awareness is raised. Inasmuch as racism is not extinct, the first possibility cannot be ruled out. But from what the students have to say, the education they are getting on racial matters does not involve a great number of first-hand experiences with racist offenses.

That is the good news. The bad news is that almost one-third of the whites interviewed reported that on the basis of their own experience at Stanford, they are more suspicious of the struggle of minorities against racism. Results from the survey of the senior class support the findings of the personal interviews. Thus 57 percent of those graduating agree with the statement, "I'm tired of hearing about racism at Stanford." Almost half of them agree that "the black student leadership is made up of people with their own political agenda who are devoted to simply *seeing* racism." Although white students are more aware of the problem of racism, a large portion of them are alienated by the anti-racist efforts of blacks. "The University is providing more education on racism," observed one student, "but without much real improvement in race relations."

As noted previously, the number of students who offered descriptions of specific racist incidents that they had actually observed firsthand was very low. According to the one-on-one interviews, white students had had more experience with racism before coming to Stanford than as undergraduates at the University. Based on the observations of the students themselves, it appears that whites learn more about racism at Stanford from *hearing* abut it than by actually seeing it. Of those students, black and white, who said they were more aware of racism since coming to Stanford, 58 percent reported that conversations with their peers opened their eyes to the problem, crediting as well the racist incidents publicized by the *Stanford Daily*. Few students, however, cite personal experiences with racism or what they would consider racist behavior.

Stanford has done its part to encourage students to think and talk about racism. Beginning in 1988, the administration has included programs on minority life at Stanford, collectively called "The Fire Within," in the activities of Freshman Orientation Week. Different minority student groups have been invited to make presentations on the challenges, triumphs, and general state of affairs of their communities on campus, which have included artistic performances and speeches by minority students. Many student residences have also held discussions for freshmen on issues facing minority students. The programs are intended to reflect both the administration's commitment to increasing racial diversity in the student body and its desire to give minority groups a voice in campus life from the very beginning of a freshman's career at Stanford.

In the fall of 1989, for example, a student speaker, Laura Gomez, delivered to an audience of new graduate students a message that, in one form or another, incoming freshmen (and virtually everyone else on campus) would hear many times from leaders of the various minority groups on campus—that Stanford is a "post-European university that must be ready for a majority of California that is basically Third World." But Stanford, she said, has not met the burden of "empowering those who have too long been disenfranchised" from this nation's political and economic life, or of "adequately describing reality as long as the voices of African-Americans, Latinos, Native Americans, and Asians are excluded from this enterprise." She called on the University to recruit "a critical mass of minority scholars in all disciplines"—specifically, people of color she described as "outside scholars" who will no longer "hide beyond the facade of the objective scholar who views his work as a value-free inquiry that aims only to clarify the world rather than to change it." Decrying the "objective scholar" as "personally damaging to all of us" and as one who "does not leave room for my voice, or for the voices of people like me," she said "our scholarship and teaching [must be] subjective in terms of our position, our background and experience, and subjective in terms of what we see as the ends or purposes of our work. Thus, in choosing our research topics and methodology," she emphasized, "we can openly embrace our values and politics and, by impacting the world around us, empower ourselves and the communities from which we come."

These "welcoming talks" by minority group leaders have elicited varied reactions from freshmen. "I have a new appreciation for minorities," said one white freshman, "and I've learned more about my own stereotypes." However, criticism outnumbered praise by about three to one. Those who complained were bothered by what they regarded as inappropriate polemics in the representations on race relations. "Looking back on Freshman Orientation," reflected a white freshman, "I feel like I got here, and from about day two I was made to feel that it was me and my values that were wrong. I felt conciliatory and so I said, 'Oh, you guys are right.' . . . Having my ideas attacked and then not being able to defend them without getting in trouble—it doesn't make for a very positive environment." Another white freshman said, "When you come to Orientation, they kind of hit you over the head with it. It's like 'Hi, meet your roommate. Don't be a racist.'"

It is hardly surprising that more than three-quarters of the black students in the hour-long personal interviews, and an equal percentage of all minorities in the senior-class survey, reported some firsthand experience with racism prior to coming to Stanford. And yet, even with so much previous exposure to racist sentiments and behavior, almost half of the blacks said their views on racism had changed while they were students at the University. Clearly, some kind of "education in racism" had taken place in the black community as well—due in large part, the black students said, to interaction with their peers (about one-quarter specifically mention conversations with black upperclassmen) as well as to programs and dorm discussions in Ujamaa. It appears that blacks learn more about racism from their peers than from actual racist offenses they experience at the University.

An important phase of that education involves the special definition of racism used by a large number of black students and the Black Student Union—as noted earlier, the systemized oppression of minorities by the race in power and, in particular, the institutionalization of racial structures and prejudice geared to protect domination by whites. "I've become more aware of the definition that's used among blacks and in dorm presentations," said a black freshman living in Ujamaa. "There's more of a distinction between racism and prejudice. Minorities can't be racist because to be racist you have to have power." Another black resident spoke about the "Afro-American Studies definition of racism" which he characterized as "bigotry with power." He went on to say that many times in the dorm "blacks have shared the definition with me, saying that it comes from the Afro-American Studies Department and the black community seems to have adopted it."

The influence of Stanford's Afro-American Studies Department is perhaps best exemplified by a series of discussions on black community issues presented by black campus leaders during the 1989 fall quarter. Loosely titled the Afro-American Studies Hour, it generally involved representatives from the Afro-American Studies Department. Billed as "Racism on Campus: How We Experience It and How We Deal With It," the forum centered on comments from members of the black community—two students, one campus administrator, a dean from Stanford's Memorial Church, and the acting chair of the Afro-American Studies Department, Sylvia Wynter, who gave a mini-lecture on racism in the Western world. The assistant dean of student affairs and former vice-chair of the University Committee on Minority Issues moderated the discussion. Attired in modern Afro-American garb, she opened the forum with some observations on how the media mistreats blacks. "There seems to be a concerted effort in this country to get whites to fear young black males," she charged.

Offering a common expression of black frustration on campus and an attack on American racism and "white supremacy," all of the participants left little doubt that they shared a theoretical framework in which the problem of racism was viewed and understood. Floyd Thompkins, a recently appointed associate dean of the chapel, reflected on his life's experience with racism and how it has evolved in the past two decades. While growing up in Florida, he had to "run for his life" from the Ku Klux Klan. Racism was, to him, a fact of life. He spoke of the forms of economic oppression and subjugation he saw around him in the racist community in which he lived. "Until recently," he explained, "racism was a secondary issue and survival was first." Today, he believes, racism manifests itself in new and more subtle ways. "Nowadays on campus, racism is having to prove oneself—feeling like nobody takes you seriously." Thompkins described a "control-by-inclusion" phenomenon that characterizes what he sees as the race situation on campus: "I feel more powerless now because I must perpetuate the myth that I am part of the team. It was easier when I was excluded, because everything was clear." As an example, he said that when he arrived at Stanford the administrators responsible for his appointment gave him a list of people whom he should meet at once, virtually all of whom were people connected in some way to the ethnic-minority communities on campus. "Their sense of my agenda," Thompkins lamented, "involved only the racial-ethnic enclave. My qualifications were restrictively defined in terms of a ministry focused on minorities and no one else." Although given a position in the system, he was controlled within an imposed framework of expectations on the part of the

Stanford administration.

Mary Hanes, then working as a campus administrator in Stanford's Office of Residential Affairs, described herself as a black Chicano. A 1983 Stanford graduate, she once held a position as a recruiter of black students for the University and was later very much involved in Stanford's Western Culture debate. Hanes spoke of the need for the full expression of black and Hispanic cultures on campus. The crux of her statement was her description of an allegedly racist incident she experienced while still a student. At a discussion about the media, Hanes asked one of the speakers, a reporter, about the way minorities are treated in the press. The reporter responded by talking about black people in the media, at which point, Hanes recalled, "I said to him, 'That was so blatantly racist. You just knocked out so many other races by only talking about blacks. Because I look black, you've cut out a whole half of me. That's racism.'" Evidently because she looks African-American rather than Hispanic, Hanes saw the reporter's decision to talk only about blacks rather than all minorities as an attack on all non-black ethnic groups.

Canetta Ivy, a senior, had been active in the Black Student Union since her freshman year. She was also a former member of the student Council of Presidents, running on the minority-dominated Peoples' Platform ticket. By her own account, she grew up (in Houston, Texas) "believing there was no racism." It was not something she expected to find when she arrived at Stanford in the autumn of 1986. "But I came here not having a very strong 'self.' There was a lot of self-hate, perpetuated by the portrayal of blacks in the media. I came here thinking that to be black was a terrible thing, especially to be a light-skinned black." She immediately felt the pressure of being an "ambassador for her race," a task for which she said she was ill-equipped. "People were telling me that my culture had nothing to offer. I said we did, but I didn't know what"—not because anybody ever told her that her culture had nothing to offer, but because of existing conditions at the University and, she noted in particular, the state of the Western Culture requirement. "I was very involved in the Western Culture debate. They acted like Afro-Americans had contributed nothing, and I knew that was wrong. I didn't know what they had contributed, but I knew we had an important place."

As did many other black students, Ivy sought refuge from the doubts she felt about herself by retreating deep into the black community on campus. "I joined every black organization I could. I wanted nothing but black people around me. I wanted black everything." Gradually, she explained, she became more aware of the merits of her culture and more sensitized to the challenges of being black at Stanford. "The subtle things I've started to pick up, but part of me is afraid of people thinking I'm hypersensitive." She described two racist incidents she had experienced, one before she entered the University, the other on campus. The first was in a crowded restroom in Memphis, where all the women were obliged to stand in line to use the sinks and to share each sink bowl with another woman. She watched as one woman washed her hands, and then proceeded to wash the hands and face of her daughter. Ivy stood in line behind a few white women and watched as they shared the sink with the woman and her daughter. But when she walked up to wash her hands, the woman picked up her daughter and moved to another sink in an obvious gesture of disapproval.

The second experience involved the staff at Stanford's Green Library. At the library exit there is a bag inspection booth designed to keep students from walking away with materials they have not checked out. Ivy watched as the several white students ahead of her were waved on by the inspector. She was stopped, however, and her bags were checked. "Just because I'm black," she claimed, "that guy thought I was going to steal some books."[2] As for fighting racism, she said she "tries to find things in my culture to be proud of. I find a lot of support," she added, "in the unity among blacks at Stanford."

The other student panelist was John Heinman, a junior and an important figure in the black community who played a big role in forming the Afro-American Studies Hour. Declining to share racist experiences out of his own background and his years at Stanford, he addressed the problem as if it were an obvious "given" and proceeded to outline his theories. He too appeared to have been profoundly influenced by what he had learned from the Afro-American Studies Department. It was as if he had taken some of the theoretical constructs and adapted them to his life as a black student and leader at the University— in a word, infused academic theory with the bitter taste of personal experience. Some of his verbatim observations require little elaboration:

I see a fallacy in the term "racism." I prefer "white supremacy."

In the term racism, there should be the idea that you have the power to accomplish your aims.

There is no such thing as reverse racism, reverse sexism, because those people don't have the wherewithal to act out their prejudices.

White supremacy is dangerous because it is subtle.

On the poor academic performance of blacks:
I think many black Americans internalize white supremacy. It has manifested itself in academic performance.

On Western culture:
Europeans have cultivated for many hundreds of years the framework in which we act, and that framework has been bent on perpetuating white supremacy. If blacks are fighting blacks,

we've got to look at how that perpetuated white supremacy. If blacks are fighting Hispanics, we've got to look at how that perpetuated the system.

White supremacy is something I deal with twenty-four hours a day [because] it's so intertwined in the fabric of how this society thinks.

Heinman's proposed solutions to the problem were far-reaching. "I suggest we look at white supremacy in a more holistic or dialectical sense, as opposed to reductionist thinking," he said, indicating that he did not support "spot fire" policymaking. Any solution to racism, he insisted, cannot come in the form of specific policies geared to specific racial issues. Nothing short of revolution will eradicate the problem. "We should adopt new language because the language we use to communicate with whites is a product of white supremacy." The revolution, in short, must come in the way blacks think about racism—"in the categories of consideration that necessarily involve the very language we use to address the problem."

Prof. Wynter, explaining her radical opinions with a torrent of allegorical examples, swept away many of the socio-scientific concepts on which modern Western culture is built. Arguing that Westerners assigned to race the quality of "status organization," she said that "when we talk about the race situation today, we are content to build on that corrupt foundation." In a sense, she maintained, "we all must be racist because we operate in a classifying system." It is the classification itself that is the problem. Man, as a social creature, must seek a means by which to organize his social group. Throughout the ages he has done it through an "us versus them" mentality. "To maintain a certain social cohesion," she said, "men must maintain and perpetuate the concept of a pariah class, which is consistently identified as an enemy." Race quite naturally grew to be the salient "social totem," for genetic differentiation was most obvious through skin color. Thus Western society had secured for itself a convenient outcast group. The people of Africa and the Americas were perceived as "raw," "putrid," and "dangerous," whereas the Europeans saw themselves as representing "purity, safety, and culture." Whiteness, explained Professor Wynter, could take the place of being French or Slavic "and becomes a cohering principle only by excluding nonwhites."

Wynter's message (as also revealed in an interview with the *Stanford Daily*) becomes quickly evident: There is a desperate need to revolutionize traditional academic disciplines to account for issues of race. Contending that America is "primarily ordered by race, with white and black at the extremes," she asserts that the real distinction is between black and white. All the other differences grow out of this basic difference. According to Wynter, when people attack the West on issues like ethnic studies, multiculturalism, and Afrocentrism, they view the debates from a Western perspective. "What we are calling multiculturalism is really the term for an enormous problem. It is also very dangerous. In multiculturalism," she points out, "you equate the nonwhite groups with the white groups, with the former now bidding for cultural hegemony and trying to displace the WASPs." Thus she does not believe that racism can be changed by what she calls a "counterinsurgency of multiculturalism," a notion that in her view is founded on the culture-bound misunderstanding that American society is an amalgam of many distinctive groups that have their own unique cultures. "If the United States didn't live within one cultural model, how could it survive?" Wynter asks. "What we have is a single American culture that expresses itself in various forms according to the history of a social group." She maintains that by attacking the problem of racism with an agenda for ethnic identification, we have perpetuated the system of totemic racial stigmatisms that generated the problem in the first place. She asks the rhetorical question: "Why should race and ethnicity be salient divisions in our society?" To rid ourselves of the burden of racism, we must set aside the "natural sociological impulse" to replicate a stable order that is based on perpetuating "a system of pariahs and dominants."

Wynter contends that with society having entered the Technological Age, the information explosion has created a need for every student attending college today to be broadly educated. "It is essential that we have a group of people who are capable of understanding the requirements of our increasingly complex society. Affirmative action, multicultural curricula—it's like bailing water on the Titanic. We no longer need that," she complains. "The first thing people are doing is trying to patch up the system, which is where we get affirmative action. Really, the whole system is an anachronism." The time is ripe for fundamental change—"a wholesale revolution in knowledge" equivalent to the revolution that liberated science from the restrictions of theology in the Middle Ages. She calls for an end to the "status-organizing principles of race," which necessarily involves a change in our very conception of race. She hopes that Americans will now begin to ascribe to the philosophy of humanity, that we shall "identify ourselves as humans rather than this race or that people." Her own utopia is a social order without the "other," without a "them" in the "us versus them." To end racism, race must no longer be the emblem or symbol of social organization. Rather than an "ad hoc multiculturalism," she hopes for a great monoculturalism that decisively extinguishes the meaningless concept of ethnicity. She does not support those who urge dropping the "melting pot" image in favor of the "salad bowl" (as Stanford president Donald Kennedy has done in welcoming incoming freshmen). "The problem that confronts us is integrating all Americans, and doing it consciously"—in a word, integration, not desegregation, and overt inclusion in American culture, not merely racial or group apportionment.

It is ironic that Prof. Wynter's ideas, so influential in the rhetoric of race relations as frequently adopted not only by the leaders of the Black Student Union, but by many black and white Stanford students, have at the same time been so misunderstood as the battle lines over racism have been drawn. These individuals seem to have borrowed Wynter's notion that in Western society race became the prominent social totem that led to America's securing for itself a convenient pariah class, but only to convert this theory for their own purposes into the more politically useful concept of pervasive white supremacy. They also seem, however, to have omitted her principal contention that the best way to solve the problem of racism is to put an end to the consideration of racial division in any form.

◄ 5 ►

How Blacks and Whites Get Along

A n alumnus of Stanford and, during his undergraduate years, a careful observer of race relations on campus reports an incident from his own adolescence that helped him to identify what he terms "a basic difference in understanding between black and white students."

For fourteen-year-old males, P.E. classes are the testing grounds for nascent masculinity. With that in mind, the coach had devised a game called matball. It was made for fourteen-year-old boys. We covered the gym with wrestling mats, chose up teams, crowded together in the center, and got down on all fours—no one was allowed to stand up during the game. The coach would toss a red rubber playground ball into the heart of that pool of eager, excited youngsters, and we'd swarm to it like piranha after an open wound. The idea was for a team to somehow get the ball to their end of the gym without a member of the team being "dog-piled" while in possession of the ball.

Though I was small for my age and very thin, I was something of an athlete and was therefore always a team captain. My nemesis in the P.E. class was a boy named Tom. In objective terms, Tom was huge. In the eyes of a scrawny adolescent, he was titanic. But in this game I had the advantage, for matball was really a game of agility. One needed strength to fight off tacklers, but the key to winning was to be able to pass the ball to a teammate before the "dog-pile" was upon you. Tom, always the other captain, picked his friends for his team, and they were all almost as big as he was. I was free to choose the small quick fellows, and my team always won.

Eventually, Tom got sick of it, and he did what was required by code—he stopped the game one day and threatened to turn my body inside out. The coach stepped in and stayed my execution, but the gauntlet had been thrown. Tom's threats continued, his friends were intimidating my teammates, and the coach started bringing his first-aid kit to class. A few days later we changed the rules of the game to make things more fair. We started playing with a large canvas ball full of sand. But Tom and I had learned the pattern of hostility. The game was increasingly equitable, but the atmosphere of the class was increasingly tense. Tom and I learned to compete like men, but we competed against one another. Our relationship was only restored a long while later when we played football together and were forced into teamwork.

Although the analogy is far from perfect, the story nonetheless illustrates the simple point that even if the situation (in this case a game of matball) is made more just and fair, opposing players do not necessarily get along better. Put very simply, the struggle against racism and the push for better race relations are two different things. For many in the black student community, racism is an issue of power. Stanford's Western Culture debates, which drew national headlines, were a great witness to black power on campus. After the Western Culture track was revised to include more non-European authors, someone asked the president of the Black Student Union what was next. "Anything we want," he answered. Race relations, on the other hand, involve basic skills and dealings in individual and group interaction. In short, blacks' concern with power and control does not assure the promotion or attainment of interracial unity.

The differences between blacks and whites in their approaches to the problem of racism are played out in the arena of social relationships in very real and important ways. White students, as already noted, are frustrated by the way in which black students try to bring about changes at Stanford. They are especially concerned about what they feel is the desire and effort of a large number of blacks to keep themselves apart from the rest of the University community. Although none of the established fraternities and sororities may exclude anyone from membership on the basis of race or color, there are half a dozen all-black fraternities and sororities. Moreover, after the Beethoven incident, in which two white freshmen hung a racially offensive poster in the Afro-American theme house, a grassroots movement by a segment of the black community called for an all-black dormitory. Stanford students are generally articulate, socially adept, and more self-confident than most, which is why it is not surpris–ing that large percentages of them—from all groups and back–grounds—report that they are comfortable in dealing with those of different races. Yet this comfortableness in interracial interaction, as many of them acknowledge, does not extend far beyond casual relating.

Despite all the problems in race relations and what is frequently characterized as "pervasive racial anxiety," surface conditions between blacks and whites are very good—and certainly much better than many of the general accounts in the press would lead one to believe. In a letter to the *Stanford Daily*, a student wrote, "In spite of the many things that have been said about racial tension at Stanford, the real news is that most people on campus are fair to all racial and ethnic groups." That statement was reprinted in the senior survey, and close to two-thirds of the graduating class agreed. Over one-third of the white students in the hour-long interviews believe that whites and minorities on campus interact "a lot"; another 35 percent said "some." Half of the blacks say that whites and minorities have "a lot" of interaction. Furthermore, over three-quarters of the blacks say they feel "very comfortable" in relating to white students, and an even larger percentage feel that whites are "very comfortable" or "somewhat comfortable" in relating to them. The University Committee on Minority Issues (UCMI) concluded that nine out of ten Stanford students feel "quite" or "very" comfortable with those of other races or backgrounds. And the results from the senior survey are similar, with a solid 86 percent rating black-white relations as "fair" or "good" (though only 3 percent said they were "excellent").

Most interracial interactions seem to take place in the dormitories. The UCMI reported that students "met friends primarily in their living groups, and secondarily through other friends." In the personal interviews, 40 percent of the students also said that whites and minorities interact most frequently in the dorms, rather than in social functions such as parties and sporting events. Although there is reason to believe that interracial dating on campus creates some tension, the UCMI confirmed that about half of the whites had dated interracially and that the proportion of blacks who had done so was as high as 75 percent.

These are encouraging numbers, showing clearly that in recent years Stanford has experienced heartening developments in interracial relations. But to emphasize only the ample number of cross-racial acquaintances and the healthy degree of comfort Stanford students enjoy with one another would be to present an incomplete picture. The more complicated truth is that interracial interaction does not appear to occur at significant levels of friendship. Relationships are often reserved and circumspect, restrained by apathy, fears, and a certain amount of peer pressure. Despite their social skills and general friendliness, many students do not relate exceptionally well or become close personal friends with other individuals of different races or ethnic groups. On the community level, whites and blacks encounter barriers that make interracial interaction even more difficult. In the course of conversations with students, it was frequently volunteered that blacks and whites do not interact in any significant way on a social level. Virtually all of the students interviewed who live in Ujamaa, the Afro-American theme house—a place where blacks and whites are constantly exposed to one another—reported routine racial segregation. When students in the senior survey were asked to comment on the statement, "There is a great deal of socializing between black and white students at parties and similar events," almost 70 percent said they either "somewhat" or "strongly" disagreed.

It seems fair to say that black and white students at Stanford "get along." They attend classes together, but they do not eat together. They live in peace with each other—"we coexist," as one student put it—but they do not fully integrate in the most positive sense of the term. As another student remarked, "We may learn a bit *about* each other, but we probably won't learn much *from* each other."

A large majority of students from all racial groups said that blacks segregate themselves from the rest of the campus community. The statistics are overwhelming. Of the students interviewed, most of the whites believe that minorities, chiefly blacks, separate themselves from whites. The same was true for most of the black students. Almost nine out of ten white students perceived separate minority social spheres (again chiefly black) and most of them felt those spheres were closed to whites. Generally speaking, blacks were even more likely than whites to think that black students voluntarily isolate themselves from whites on campus. A sizable percentage identify an impulse among their peers to remain apart from the wider Stanford community, in large part because of the blacks' need, as one black student observed, "to fit into black social circles." Almost 70 percent of the blacks talked of the pressure they felt from other black students to subscribe to a set of "black" positions and attitudes. "Oh yeah, that's everywhere," said a black sophomore. "It involves certain standards that you're supposed to adopt." A black freshman pointed out that "there are some things a real black person does not do. For instance, you have to dress 'black'." A black junior added that "loud laughing, more aggressive displays of emotion, I guess—that's different than what whites do. There are certain modes of behavior. We're told not to forget who we are."

The UCMI found that "a substantial proportion of minority students indicated they must make extra efforts to be accepted by those from their same racial/cultural background." Ninety percent of the black students reported feeling the need to make such efforts, and the Committee concluded that one-third of the blacks agreed to some extent that they felt "pressured to participate in ethnic activities at Stanford." In the personal interviews with black students, a large number of them said that social affiliation with whites cuts down their acceptance by their peers. "If you hang around with just white people, you might get dropped in status," noted one black student. Well over three-fourths of those in the senior survey who offered opinions on the subject agreed that blacks feel pressure to avoid close friendships with whites. Several of the blacks who were interviewed went so far as to call this form of black separatism "reverse racism toward whites." Some were openly discouraged by the situation. One black freshman said, "Before, when someone did something wrong to me, race never crossed my mind as the reason. But then I had to change my way of thinking about people. I had to start worrying about the way they saw me because I'm black. I didn't want to change the way I saw people, but it's hard when all the blacks are saying beware this and beware that."

A survey done by Stanford Research Institute International for the UCMI determined that roughly 80 percent of the black students on campus had at least one good friend ("someone with whom you share your problems and joys and spend time with socially") of a different race. It appears, however, that blacks approach such friendships with caution. SRI International also found that blacks were unique among campus minorities in that they are more likely to have friends of the same race than they are to have non-minority friends. And while as many as half of the black students had dated interracially, most of them indicated that interracial dating reduced their approval from black colleagues. It is perhaps worth noting that no white student said mixing socially with blacks would meet with disfavor by his or her friends or in any way damage that student's social standing. In the senior survey, almost everyone disagreed with the statement, "There is pressure here on white students—from other whites—to avoid developing close friendships with black students."

There is little disagreement that blacks segregate themselves from whites at Stanford. "Ask me why and my answer begins with our history of subjugation," explained a member of the Black Student Union. "Whites have had the power ever since this country got started, and they abused it. The rest of my answer is that they still have the power and they still abuse it. How do you fight against the misuse of power? With your own power," he said. "At a university like this, you fight against being manipulated by the system by gaining control yourself. For black students, a place managed by blacks is a safe place, free from the racial slurs and suspicion that exist everywhere else on campus. Also," he added, "in black-controlled arenas blacks are freed from the pressure to evaluate themselves in comparison with whites. This, I can assure you, is a serious matter in the black community."

In the personal interviews, a number of blacks spoke of "feeling the burden of comparison with whites," a burden that sometimes gets so heavy that they try to escape the pressure by withdrawing into their own social circles. Comparisons take place on many levels. One of the biggest and most worrisome concerns of blacks is that whites are the ones who are making the comparisons and arriving at judgments about the academic abilities of black students. Roughly one in five whites interviewed believed that minority freshmen are less academically qualified to be at Stanford than white students. But even more blacks—approximately 30 percent—believed the same thing. UCMI figures show that almost one quarter of them felt "less prepared for Stanford academically than most Stanford students," compared to 16 percent of the white students. Four times as many blacks as whites thought that if they let up very much on their studying, they would "probably end up on academic probation."

The degree to which many blacks lack confidence in their academic abilities is further underscored in the one-on-one interviews, where a great many of them said they felt that doubts about their competence are widely held on campus. For example, over 40 percent thought that the faculty expected less from them than from white students. A black sophomore said, "I've had teachers in classes say, 'Does everybody understand?', and then they'll ask me specifically and the other blacks. They just kind of assume that we don't." The UCMI concluded that "many minority students are particularly disturbed to hear their academic legitimacy at Stanford questioned." But, as one white student observed, "We have affirmative-action programs that place a priority on admitting minorities. Well, you just have to believe that some minorities that are here wouldn't have gotten in if there were no affirmative action." Most of the seniors surveyed agreed with the statement, "Merit, not race or color, should be the predominant factor in Stanford's admissions process." Yet the interviews also reveal that few whites actually have serious doubts about the academic performance of black students. Of the 20 percent of whites who thought that minorities are less qualified when they enter Stanford, three-quarters said that given time, minority students easily make up ground academically.

In short, while most white students are wary of affirmative-action policies, relatively few of them seem to believe there are many blacks at Stanford who are academically unqualified to succeed. The key issue, however, is the perception blacks themselves have of what whites believe—and what many blacks sense, as one black student put it, is that "whites don't think we measure up." Blacks also realize that some of them are beneficiaries of affirmative action, which only serves to heighten their sensitivity to anything (or anyone) that might place their academic talents in a less than favorable light. "That's a heavy load to carry," observes a faculty member, "and they sometimes try to escape the pressure by withdrawing into their own social circles."

For their part, white students are frustrated and fearful. They are frustrated by the self-seclusion of blacks. Very few of them define racism in terms of oppression, subjugation, and the battle of race against race. They regard racism as much more a matter of unhealthy stereotyping and generalizing about individuals and groups of a different race or ethnic background. Although most students were not alive when the civil-rights struggles of the 1960s began, they know that Martin Luther King Jr. had a dream that one day blacks and whites would be able to sit down "at the table of brotherhood." They are disappointed that his dream, as one white student commented, "has failed to become an important part of the action agenda of the black community on campus." About 70 percent of the white students interviewed believe that whites are generally supportive of the goals and aspirations of blacks. Why then, they ask, does the black leadership talk so much about white hostility? Why the talk of black power and white oppression? Why do blacks separate themselves into their own "territorial units"? Most white students interpret separatism as an unprovoked and undeserved act of hostility on the part of the black community, and, in their frustration, do not know how to respond.

Whites are also fearful. Racism is a burning issue at Stanford, as it is on other campuses, and the term "racist" is intimidating. Whites do not want to be considered racist. Although they often resent what they perceive as the aggressive verbal attacks and confrontational spirit of the black community, whites are sincere in wanting black students to feel comfortable at Stanford. They do not understand why so many black students seem to find the campus an ungenerous and inhospitable environment. Blacks' tendency to seclude themselves appears to whites as confirmation that blacks (or a sizable number of them) prefer isolation from the wider campus. Moreover, many students who have associated with blacks frequently admit that they have been haunted by the fear of doing or saying something wrong. "I'm scared to be called racist," said one student in a group interview in one of the dorms. "You've really got to be careful all the time." Another student stated that the word "racist" is so powerful an accusation that it gets used as a political weapon by minority groups, adding that "the motivation is often too little and the risk too great to spend the energy required to bridge a culture gap in interpersonal relations."

The importance of "culture" crops up repeatedly in interviews with both black and white students. Quick to acknowledge that ethnic and group differences are an essential part of the rich and varied history of the United States, white students frequently stress the need to listen to a "diversity of voices" in order to understand fully the uniqueness of our common experience as a democratic society. They also support the concept of cultural pluralism, which has reshaped the way many faculty members define liberal education today.

At the same time, however, the idea of multiculturalism has taken a new turn. Increasingly the talk among black students is about cultural differences—more specifically, about reinforcing and maintaining a distinct cultural identity, sometimes by calling for separate living quarters or a more ethnocentric curriculum (or both) that, they insist, are needed not only to raise blacks' self-esteem but to strengthen their bases of power in the University and ultimately free themselves of the racism of American culture. When asked to describe black culture, black students often speak of the differences in black humor or (the category most frequently cited) "black English." As one black sophomore noted, "When we get together we talk in certain dialects, I guess you could call them. White people could understand it, but black people talk it." Some blacks explain black culture in more personal terms. "It has a lot to do with who you *feel* you have common bonds with," said a black freshman. "Our backgrounds are mainly similar. We like the same things." Another black freshman described one way that a concern for black culture is translated into self-segregation: "I don't mind if a black person wants to date a white person," he said. "What bothers me is the motivation. Society has given us the message that blacks can only help ourselves, and that's compromised when black men see white women as something better. If black people do not share a distinct, separate culture, there will be some real problems."

Since the earliest stirrings of the civil-rights movement in the late 1950s and early 1960s, it was clear that a positive, prideful understanding of their own identity as black Americans was an explicit part of their long and hard struggle for freedom and equality. Dr. King had set the tone by proclaiming the new freedom that was close at hand—the freedom to be black without shame because the color of one's skin would no longer be an obstacle to high achievement and self-fulfillment. From the day he began the bus boycott in Montgomery, black identity became synonymous with a new black dignity. But today, as a black senior observed, "black pride has a different meaning, because there's a new definition of blackness." He talks of the "learning process" that blacks are experiencing on campus as they work out for themselves what it means to be "black at Stanford," and of how many blacks "will pay special attention to the things that set them apart as a distinct social group"—as others have also done, he mentions language, humor, social conduct, even music. Separateness, he wants us to understand, can become an important value for blacks—not necessarily as an end in itself, but as part of the exercise of defining "who we are and what we may become." In this regard, it should be noted that in a UCMI survey roughly 85 percent of blacks agreed that their "racial/ethnic heritage is a central part of [their] sense of identity." Black students, in short, clearly have as part of their personal self-awareness a strong consciousness of their blackness.

A long-time leader in the black community at Stanford (who has also held an administrative position at the University) explains that "today's students didn't live through the 1960s like I did. They've got to figure out in their own way what all this stuff about racism and blackness means for them. As for me, I want people to see me as a person first and a black man second. But can folks be that color-blind," he asks, "if the first thing new students see when they get here is 'The Fire Within' (the Freshman Orientation program), which encourages students to be acutely aware of color differences?" White students, many of whom come to Stanford from a background of limited exposure to minorities, immediately learn to view black students in a unique manner, he observes, "and black students, through early presentations by the Black Recruitment and Orientation Committee and the Black Student Union, immediately learn that their blackness will be an important part of who they are on campus." The black leaders on campus who are responsible for the programs of ethnic awareness, he says, "do not believe that we should have only a *secondary* awareness of racial differences." They want students at Stanford to be fully aware of their racial identity; an important part of their campus mission is to teach that lesson to whites and other blacks who do not already agree. As a black columnist for the *Stanford Daily* wrote, "I think I can speak for many other blacks when I say that the key is not in viewing all minorities as whites, but in realizing that minorities are different from whites." A black junior living in Ujamaa maintained that "in color-blindness, you're trying to de-culture people. People should be different but equal." Interracial dating is dangerous, explained another black student, "because it could end up compromising the black family and lead to a loss of racial identity." What might be called an identity rooted in cultural difference and social segregation has come to be valued highly by many black students, which perhaps may make it easier to understand why most of the blacks who were interviewed agreed that any official Stanford policy of color-blindness would be a form of prejudice.

An additional dimension to the concern over the differences between blacks and whites is that some black students feel—and resent—the burden of educating whites. The UCMI reported that black students "who don't want to play the role of 'ethnic ambassador' can find this situation trying and difficult." As one black woman said to the Committee, "My freshman year I had people coming around to me. . . . When there is an issue of ethnicity . . . then all of a sudden I'm the ambassador, I'm the most knowledgeable person. And they come to me, and they want an answer." This can become a difficult problem. White students entering Stanford as freshmen learn right away that blacks want to be viewed as blacks, that there are important differences between the black and white communities on campus, and that they must be sensitive to those differences. Often, however, specific differences remain ill defined.

What is clear is that a large section of the black community segregates itself. Whites who care enough to learn more about ethnic differences approach blacks in their dormitories, but frequently discover that blacks feel pressured when asked to speak in behalf of their race. The situation calls for great sensitivity on the part of whites, and a good deal of patience by blacks. As one graduating white senior observed, "I would guess that if blacks and whites were really comfortable with each other at the outset, communication about ethnic differences would be easier. After all, students are good at finding answers to unspoken questions through the whole process of making friends." But as we have seen, blacks and whites do not as a rule have significant relationships developed through long association. That blacks feel pressured when put in the position of having to talk about or explain themselves is perhaps another reason for the relative absence of close and enduring friendships—or, conversely, it might simply be a symptom of the lack of intimacy and trust between black and white students.

Meanwhile, the separation continues, largely because a significant number of blacks regard the problem of racism on campus not as an issue of interpersonal relations between whites and blacks but as a struggle for power by blacks to change the system of white control at Stanford. Thus the blacks' demands for more black students on the Board of Trustees, more black faculty members, more classes about their history and culture taught by blacks—these have all been attempts to win a solid place in the academic structure of the University. As already mentioned, however, the blacks' pursuit of power does not presuppose improvements in interracial relationships. After the incident in Ujamaa, for example, the Students of Color Coalition demanded that Stanford drop the requirement that the student population living in Ujamaa must be at least 50 percent nonblack. The call was for more black control, not for greater interracial understanding, for more power to protect blacks rather than for education and reconciliation. Virtually without exception, all formal declarations made by black organizations in recent years have had as their paramount goal increased black power on campus. And with each advance in the fight for institutional change comes affirmation of the power that the black community has accrued for itself as a separate social entity. Moreover, in the awareness of their strength-through-separateness has also come further validation for black students of their unique and positive ethnic identity.

But at what cost, ask many white students? As race relations are routinely reduced to power equations, black and white students "will never relate easily and freely on a large scale," observes a white senior. "It's entirely too easy to see power as a zero-sum game, which almost precludes any expectation of cooperation and mutual enhancement."

In much the same way that blacks perceive that whites have doubts about their academic ability, whites perceive that blacks see them as racists. This perception is aggravated when whites, or the "white system," are explicitly blamed for the oppression of blacks on campus. Most white students do not agree with the charge that racial oppression is inherent in Stanford's power structure—almost 60 percent of the seniors believe that the administration has been very sensitive to the concerns of black students—and even if some of them might think the University should demonstrate more understanding, they do not think that, as individuals, they must automatically share in the guilt. In point of fact, a fairly large percentage of white students *are* willing to share in a very general way the guilt assigned to all whites because of the pernicious treatment accorded to blacks in our nation's history. In the senior survey, almost half of the white students agreed that "whites must live with the knowledge that they are responsible for the discrimination and prejudice blacks face today." Yet in every instance when white students were asked about specific race-related occurrences on campus, such as the Beethoven incident at Ujamaa, they were not willing to accept responsibility. They also rejected any suggestion that all white students should be grouped with those actually responsible every time a racial incident occurs.

It is clear that whites want to be judged as individuals, and that most whites do not believe they have personally done anything to perpetuate a racist system. Nor do they accept the implicit message they see in black separatism that all whites are not to be trusted. Apart from feeling that they can and deserve to be trusted, they resent the fact that at the same time that blacks are adamant in opposing racism, they continue to segregate themselves from whites. Self-segregation is precisely the kind of action and behavior that whites consider discriminatory. But a great many blacks, inclined to think of racism in institutional terms and therefore as firmly fixed in the University, insist that the real problem is oppression, not segregation.

These are fundamental disparities. Almost 60 percent of the graduating class of 1989 agreed that "Stanford should emphasize what students have in common, not their differences." In the personal interviews, nine out of ten whites said that minority organizations highlight the differences between ethnic groups and races, and most of them thought this was an unhealthy development. In contrast, while most blacks agreed that minority organizations like the Black Student Union underline racial differences, only a small number of them felt it was a problem. Many white students, however, are convinced, as one junior commented, that "only a minority of blacks are extreme. I don't think a lot of people out there wholeheartedly agree with the polemics of the BSU, or think that the BSU represents more than the views of those who are the activists, or who live in Ujamaa." A white senior said, "There are two black populations at Stanford: the blacks who are 'into' their own culture in a big way, and those who aren't 'into' it so much. It seems like the vocal minority is causing the problem." Other whites described some situations as "safer" than others. "When I talk to those blacks who separate themselves in the dining hall simply as individuals," a white freshman pointed out, "there's no trouble. It's just when they're all together that they consider me white."

The result of all this, it seems, is interracial tension. Seventy percent of those in the senior survey agreed with the statement, "Racial tension on campus has increased in the years I've been on campus." According to many observers, the rise in tension is due to the growing number of racial incidents at Stanford, or even across the country. It is certainly true that racism is discussed more frequently today than in the past at student dining tables, in study groups, and on the front pages of the newspapers, suggesting that in some part the increased tension is a function of the widespread attention given to the whole issue. Yet it is difficult to say if the rising tension is a result of the polarization between blacks and whites on campus, or whether the polarization is the result of the higher level of tension. The answer most likely would be different for each group, or even for each individual. For reasons of culture, racial identity, and self-perception, many blacks believe they have good reason to separate themselves. Whites, on the other hand, feel thwarted by blacks' separatism, worry about being called racist, and are angered by what they perceive as reverse racism. "One thing I can say for sure," observed a white senior, "is that the form of racial segregation that exists at the University has done very little to ease the tension at all." In the interviews done by Pacific Management Systems for the UCMI, a resounding 95 percent of blacks reported feeling that they do not fit into the Stanford community. And the interviews conducted by the Strategic Research Institute determined that 40 percent of blacks feel they must minimize their ethnic characteristics to fit in.

But why? Why, in a university that is nationally known for its major commitment to ethnic diversity in the student body and the curriculum, do so many blacks not fit in? Why, with large ethnic organizations, ethnic theme houses, ethnic-studies programs, new courses in the philosophy of the Third World, and new Freshman Orientation programs focusing on the minority experience, do they feel the campus is so unfriendly? And why are many white students leaving Stanford feeling less sympathetic to minority causes than when they entered?

By now, of course, the questions are almost rhetorical. "The main cause of our ills," commented a graduating senior, "is the continued segregation between blacks and whites. We've learned coexistence, but not understanding." When the UCMI asked students, "To what extent, if at all, has your Stanford experience improved your ability to interact comfortably with people of different racial/ethnic groups from your own?", half the blacks said "little" or "none at all." One-third of the whites agreed. Blacks may be winning structural changes in the University, but there is a strong sense that they are not winning a growing number of friends. And many whites, who may have anticipated being better prepared to live in an increasing multicultural America, leave with greater suspicion of minority communities.

◀ 6 ▶

Three Student Profiles

I.
The Black Activist

"William" is a very busy young man. Since his freshman year he has been deeply involved with different black student organizations on campus, including the Black Student Union, the Black Pre-Business Society, the Black Pre-Law Society, and the Gospel Choir. Now that he is a junior, he has assumed varying leadership roles in these organizations. Despite the heavy extracurricular load, he maintains a B average in his general course work. "I'm one of those that figures you get out of it what you put in," he explains, "and I plan to get a lot out of Stanford."

Listening to him talk, one senses that his mind

is racing ahead to anticipate the direction of the conversation, as if to prepare for the next question or argument. His words are measured, and he refuses to answer a question without being absolutely certain of its intent. Neat in appearance, his dorm room is meticulously organized. When he sits, his posture is straight and his body still, until he begins to make a point. Then he leans forward, his eyes grow wide, and his hands dart in front of him to punctuate his sentences. He is clearly a man of strong opinions.

In the large Western city in which he grew up, William learned some hard lessons in race relations. His high school had a minority enrollment of only 10 percent, but his own neighborhood was mainly black. Both of his parents worked full-time at hourly-wage jobs, together grossing about $35,000 a year. He would be the first in his family to earn a college degree.

"I had a lot of experience with racism before I got to Stanford," he says. It was a ubiquitous sort of racism that confronted him at every turn. "My parents faced discrimination in their jobs. My Dad got stuck on the lowest pay scale and was denied promotions because of his race. It was just obvious. We even started some lawsuits." His neighborhood was segregated. "There were just certain places you could live if you were black. And people used to make all kinds of racial slurs against blacks... 'Nigger this, nigger that' wherever you went." There were days when the racial hostilities exploded in violence, and the gangs on the streets waged small wars against each other. "Every once in a while," he remembers, "some guy would get beat up because he was black or white or whatever. Sometimes they'd get killed. There are places where I live where you don't go if your skin is a different color. Period."

And sometimes the violence hit closer to home. "My sister was in this after-school basketball league when she was a kid. One day a group of white kids ganged up on her and beat her up. She asked why, and they just hit her again and jeered at her."

In school, the situation was equally frustrating. "People thought if you were black the only thing you could do was sports and that was it. Teachers were always very surprised when I did well in class." He pauses for a moment and shuts his eyes. "There was one time when I got the best score on a test, and the teacher made me take it over because she was sure I had cheated. She had no proof, but I had to retake the test. There wasn't a thing I could do about it.

"In all the gifted classes, I was the only black person, and that made me different. I stuck out and everyone, teachers and students, treated me differently," he complains. "Heck, it was even hard with my black friends, because they went to a whole different set of classes. I operated in a different world—the white world. It was like I went to a different school within the same school."

William found that his successes did not always translate into greater social ease and acceptance. He counts himself one of a broad group of black Americans who have improved their socioeconomic positions without the associated rewards of confidence and respect. "Blacks are doing better in this country. You hear about the growing black middle class," he says, "but then you watch television and you see it doesn't mean much." He holds his empty hands in front of himself to underscore his point. "The cops are white, the crooks are black on the shows. And in politics, when's the last time you saw a black man standing anywhere close to Bush on TV? And remember the campaign ad that Bush ran featuring the black rapist? That's a signal from the top. America still thinks the black man is the low-life."

In every arena, around every corner, William was forced to confront the color of his own skin. It became the immutable reality in his social functions and relationships, something he could not forget. His negative experiences led him to a hostile appraisal of the way in which whites regard blacks. Having had to deal with prejudice and discrimination in school, and through the professional challenges his parents faced, he developed a race-relations theory of utility. "I think it's basically how much education you have, how much money, how well you do—that's what determines how whites view your skin color." He adds, as an afterthought, "People don't respect good ideas, but they'll respect a law degree."

But even money goes only so far. Even if blacks reach an advanced level of economic or educational status, he maintains, they still contend with an impenetrable ceiling on social status enforced through the structural biases of the white system. "Back home," he says, "I felt the place was racist, but I felt if you did better you would succeed. When I came here, I found out that even if you do better, it doesn't matter. There are people in control here, and they don't give a damn." For William, the message was clear: "If blacks can't earn respect, they must take power."

The "structural biases" at Stanford are easily discerned in their effects. "For a long time, we had no black authors in the Western Culture track—a required track that everybody takes. This was the kind of passive bias or sin of omission," he says, "that told everybody there were no blacks worth reading—no blacks that had any effect on our society." Some issues betray more-intentional discrimination. "The University has been talking about more minority faculty hiring, but they say there aren't enough minorities in the applicant pool. But if they've really been trying for twenty years to hire more blacks, you'd think they could find some worth hiring, don't you?" Other problems are a result of administrative foot-dragging. "There's no provision in the Fundamental Standard (Stanford's disciplinary policy) for prosecuting cases of racist comments and behavior that are offensive to blacks and other minorities. I say that if the University had made a decision to take racism seriously, there would already be a policy for handling it. They haven't been making black complaints a priority."

Despite his grievances about "structural racism" at Stanford, William's greatest concerns spring from his personal interactions on campus. As a part of his daily living, the most dispiriting manifestation of racism lies in the ethnic insensitivity and popular black stereotypes of his white peers. He remembers a "terrible experience" in his freshman dorm. "The white students there were incredibly insensitive to my ethnicity. You could tell by the way they acted. When I walked into a room where they were talking, they would all get quiet. One guy would try to mimic the way black people talk. They made assumptions about how much money my parents made, my academic ability, and my sexual conduct because I was black." The biggest complication was that the white students never acted blatantly racist. Their form of racism took the form of subtle behaviors and codes of relating "that only other blacks would see. That's the difficult thing," he explains. "If you point out everything they do that bothers you, they think you're hypersensitive."

William felt trapped in a Catch-22 situation in his freshman dorm. His dormmates thought their antics and remarks were funny at best and innocuous at worst. In the privacy of his own thoughts, however, William felt insulted, antagonized, and misunderstood. "There's nothing to do in a situation like that," he concludes, "except close your mouth and move on." And that's what he did. He decided to avoid white students altogether, and took shelter in the black community. Within a few weeks he practically lived in Ujamaa (the Afro-American theme house). "I hated it over there in my freshman dorm," he recalls. "I just wanted to be around black people who understood. Ujamaa has become a safe house for me."

Beginning with his sophomore year, William assumed residency in Ujamaa. The rest of his life on campus follows the pattern of segregation. "I live in a black dorm, I go to black functions and parties, I belong to a lot of black groups," he notes. He has never lived with a nonblack roommate or dated interracially. "It just simplifies life," he says. "Even if there are white students who are interested in finding out what it's like to be black, it means I always have to be explaining myself. It gets tiring, and when I come home to my room I want to be able to rest. Is that so bad?" In pursuing a restful environment he seeks both a freedom from ethnic insensitivity and a freedom to express himself in a manner that will be immediately intelligible to his black peers. "It's things that are hard to talk about, like black humor. It's different, and we laugh louder, which makes people think we're shallow and immature." He supports the simple social rule: Like likes like. As he puts it, "Only a black person knows what it's like to be raised by a black mother."

William is quiet for several moments and squints his eyes to focus his thoughts. "You know," he says finally, "when you're around only black people, nobody watches you *because* you're black." He pauses again, and proceeds cautiously: "It's not like you just fail or succeed at Stanford. You're a black who failed or a black who succeeded, you know?" He stresses the fact that belonging to a very visible ethnic minority "locks one into a game of constant comparisons—comparisons made by whites and comparisons with whites made by blacks." The black student in the majority white society is "watched and measured from all sides and from within—because he is different," he adds. Having learned that his blackness was a filter for every interaction and transaction, he quickly found out that his every achievement and setback could become a racial issue. Majority black arenas, like William's black theme house, make blacks the standard rather than the object of comparison. In a competitive university environment, he says, that is agreeably refreshing.

While his reasons for separating himself from whites were initially self-defensive, William describes the strong pressure now put on him by his black peers to remain fully segregated. "Black people don't want to socialize with any white people," he says. "They're afraid if we mix with whites we will lose our culture. It's really important not to date white people. We had this whole dorm presentation on the 'cons' of interracial dating." If he were to mingle too frequently with whites, he points out, he would suffer socially among his black peers. "They call people that hang out with whites 'miscellaneous'—not really black, you know." Being "black" involves a whole set of opinions and behavior patterns. "I guess there's a black way to dress. It's not too important, but you can't be 'new wave' or anything. There are a certain kind of glasses that are popular. They're called 'Malcolms', after Malcolm X." While dress codes are flexible, however, political views are not. "There is no way you can be a Republican and still be 'down'," he says perfunctorily. "Blacks are liberal and there's a whole set of issues with prescribed stances. I've got to admit it's pretty holistic, but we've got to think and act alike to be a community. In unity. That's the point."

For William, lessons on the value of segregation did not begin on campus. "Not all of the pressure to be black comes from around here," he observes. "Much of it comes from a mandate from home. We're told not to forget who we are." As he talks, it becomes clear that he has developed a strong historical awareness of the generations of American blacks before him, and he is conscious of the unique position in which he finds himself in the scheme of black progress. "It's like I have an opportunity they never had," he says. "Well, here I am. What am I going to do with it?" The course of recent black history has generated an obligation to do well, but also to fight against the bigotry that created the socioeconomic inequality in the first place. As William puts it, "I'm going to go places my parents couldn't go, and then wipe out all the barriers that kept them from going."

Despite his problems in dealing with the white community, William maintains he feels very comfortable relating to whites. "In my dealings with whites," he says, "I act just the way I always act." But he believes that whites are very uncomfortable relating to him. "I have the impression that most whites don't care for black males. I think they have a lot of fear when they deal with us, like they're scared of us, like they believe all the negative stereotypes they see on TV—you know, that we're all violent criminals." He tells of the time when he was campaigning for a student body office out on White Plaza. "Students who came by obviously tried to avoid me. It was comical. One girl came close to falling off her bike to stay away from me." He laughs, leans forward, and lowers his voice. "I just don't think I'm that threatening." Then he straightens up. "It seems weird to think there would be such ridiculous fear. But I swear, that's what really happened."

He talks about pressures in communicating with white students and, especially, white professors. "One problem is black English. We have a certain way of talking—a dialect," he explains. "When white people hear someone talking it, they assume that the person is not intelligent." He says he does not greatly change his behavior when dealing with whites, but he at least changes his speech. "Like when I go to see a professor. I have to make a conscious effort to speak 'proper' English. Otherwise he'll think I don't know what I'm talking about." He casts his eyes around the room and maybe recalls some episodes from his experience in his freshman dorm. "Whites think that the way we talk sounds funny, so they make fun of it, as if it's a comical language, so no one who spoke it could be serious, could be smart." Moreover, he has grown to believe that white students and professors at Stanford really are not very different from those in his high school. "Yeah, if you do well, everyone is surprised. The professors treat you differently, as if you always had a problem understanding," he complains.

Again, his perceptions of the way in which white students and professors suspect his academic qualifications are based on his observations of "subtle behavior." He admits he has actually never seen or personally experienced a blatantly racist act in a classroom, and has never observed blatantly racist behavior on the part of a faculty member. So how is it, exactly, that he is treated differently? Where is the racism? "Well, it's hard to see, but all blacks know it's there," he says. "The way profs ask you questions in class, the tone of their voice as they labor through some explanation for you. It's like they think, 'Oh, no, here's another black student who can't understand.' Heck, I've been in classes where the prof will stop the lecture to ask if students understand, and then single out blacks to ask if they're able to follow what he's saying," he says tersely. "We're singled out. Not outright embarrassed, but the implication is there, isn't it?" For his part, William says he never doubts his own abilities or those of other blacks at Stanford.

The upshot is that he believes racism is a "very serious" issue on campus, and that white students and the University administration believe differently. Accordingly, he has become an activist and combatant. "The minority groups on campus do have a political agenda," he notes. "All groups think empowerment—getting positions of power. It's all about how much power you have to get what you want. The vast majority of whites here are opposed to the black agenda. They don't want to give up the power and control they have on campus." His analysis falls in line with his definition of racism. "Racism is the oppression of people because of their race," he says. "It's a system whereby the white group in power subjugates the minority groups. That's why America is still internally drawn up along racial lines." Negative stereotypes, racial slurs, insensitive appraisals of blacks and other minorities—these are all symptoms of "a process of malicious bias," the same process "that once forced me to live in a segregated neighborhood and kept my parents shackled."

What naturally follows from this definition of racism is that any racial group not in power, and that therefore does not control the socioeconomic structures of the country, cannot be racist. "Blacks can't be racist," William explains, "because they don't have the power to actualize their prejudices. They're not part of the power base in this society." He notes that since coming to Stanford, he has come to recognize the difference between racism and prejudice. "Prejudice is just individuals hating one another for reasons of skin color. It can't oppress and subjugate people. Racism can." He acknowledges that much of what he has learned about "what racism really is" has resulted from his involvement in the Black Student Union, which he says is the voice of the black community on campus. "The BSU is absolutely right in the demands they make and in what they say, especially in agitating for institutional change in the University administration and in the curriculum," William states. "I'd give the BSU an eleven on a scale from one to ten." He pauses for a long instant, thinking carefully about what he is going to say next.

They [the BSU] talk a lot about how blacks are different, and I guess that leads to segregation. But it's the kind of segregation that promotes an appreciation of differences. It's important to fully understand the cultural differences between blacks and whites so that we can be free of all the biases. Yes, there is a black culture at Stanford. It's in our language, our art, in our music. In large part it's an issue of our race, a group of people who are and have been separated. If blacks separate themselves on campus, it's because we need to feel safe from racist feelings and attitudes we get from white relationships.

People come down on black groups because they talk so much about racial purity. Look, American blacks have been robbed of their culture. We know that in our history we have been stripped of our roots and our own pride. Today we want to get that back and really emphasize where we come from in a positive way. When I was growing up, I was forced to recognize my skin color whether I wanted to or not. Now I don't intend to forget it. I want to emphasize it. Black does not only denote my skin color. It also denotes my culture and heritage. People need to see that I'm black and really respect that. I'm glad I'm black. Don't penalize me for it and make all sorts of assumptions. People shouldn't be color-blind. They should be color-conscious, but not prejudiced.

William has forged for himself a certain amount of security in an environment that he perceives as hostile. He has taken refuge in black social circles and predominantly black living quarters. He works hard as a student, and plans to succeed in the professional world as a way of defending and proving himself "in a white system that is drenched with bigotry." He is fully committed to the development of a firm black identity for himself and his ethnic community, a condition that at once sets blacks apart and invites them in—by commanding cultural appreciation, and promising full inclusion structurally. Ultimately, William feels that blacks will only enjoy structural inclusion when they wrest away structural power. The battle is waged in the arena of white conscience with protests, and in educational and financial circles with the irresistible onslaught of success. What blacks need, he says, is "just a step up in the system." Thus he supports a program of minimum minority quotas in American colleges and universities—as he puts it, "Universities should be required to admit a higher level of blacks than there is in the United States, to overcompensate because we have been oppressed for so long." To that end, he says, Stanford is not fully committed to affirmative action in its admissions policy.

In general, Stanford is far too laissez-faire for his tastes. In addition to his complaints that the University's discipline policy is far too lax to deal effectively with white students' racist offenses, William is extremely angry over the administration's handling of the Beethoven incident at Ujamaa, in which two freshmen defaced a dorm poster with racist caricatures. The freshmen were kicked out of the dorm complex, but not expelled from school. "Drastic action should have been taken when the incident happened," he says. "They should have been thrown out." Still, when all is said and done, William does not accuse Stanford of being a racist institution—but neither is his opinion of the University filled with praise and enthusiasm. He grudgingly admits that the administration has conceded some changes in the curriculum and in various bureaucracies, "but only under pressure from the Black Student Union and other minority groups on campus." He sees piecemeal victories, all short of the goal of unqualified respect for black people and their culture. He and his colleagues, focused and angry, pursue power in a system that he believes is more apt to mollify blacks than to value them. If they are more free than in the past—"rehabilitated, so to speak," he says—they still carry with them a stigma they can neither overlook nor forget. "That will change only by our collective efforts to become a powerful broker on the campus. That's why we won't slow down."

II.
The Black Moderate

Playing on a very good basketball team in high school, "Anne" handled the point guard position on a squad consisting entirely of black girls. Everyone had high hopes for the team as it entered a Midwestern regional pre-tournament for the AAU national championship. The team played well, winning the second-place trophy.

By tradition, the first- and second-place teams were always sent to the national championships. But Anne's team was passed over by the officials, and the championship tournament spot was given to the third-place team. "They were all white girls," she says. "Everybody understood what was going on." As the controversy unfolded, it drew national attention as newspapers across the country reported on what had become a major incident. "We were in the middle of it. It was obvious what the officials were trying to do to us, but we wanted to go to the tournament and play." Finally, after a lot of dust had been kicked up, "some guys from the Justice Department came to straighten out the mess." They found the obligatory compromise; both Anne's team and the all-white team were sent to the tournament. AAU officials levied the appropriate reprimands and probations, and Anne and her teammates learned a hard lesson. "We just felt sort of betrayed by someone," she explains. "We worked really hard to prepare for the tournament. We earned a spot, so we had the right to go. And all of a sudden we thought, 'Hey, we can't go because a group of white people don't like the fact we're all black.'"

Anne grew up in a racially integrated suburban community a few miles outside a large Midwestern city. Both her parents have college degrees. Her father is a banker, her mother a housewife who stayed at home until her two daughters were in school, at which time she got a job in a bookstore. The annual family income today is somewhere over $50,000—"We're part of the upwardly mobile middle class, according to my sociology professor," Anne states with a smile. Her high school, which has a 50 percent minority enrollment, motivated her to go on to college, although fewer than half of her classmates did so. A practical person with a keen sense of her own strengths and weaknesses, she got into Stanford "because I worked hard, I guess. I mean, most anybody with a little intelligence could do it if they applied themselves." She pauses, perhaps thinking about what she just said. Then, in a different tone, she adds, "I'm maybe not brilliant, but I'm bright enough." Now a sophomore, she maintained a 2.8 GPA through her freshman year—"not bad, not great. Ugh, physics!" She winces at the memory of the ordeal.

"At my high school," she remembers, "some of the people got mad at me for getting into Stanford. I mean, they got higher SAT scores and maybe better grades, and they didn't get in and I did. They said it was just because I'm black." She pauses, searching for the right way to put things, and then begins again with the cadence of one who has given the speech before. "Blacks are given special breaks in admissions. I know that. But that doesn't mean I'm not qualified," she adds quickly. "Anyway, I'm here, and I'm making it." She looks away for a brief moment, then continues. "Look," she insists, "they have whites reading the freshman applications—probably upper-class whites—and what blacks write is sort of geared more towards black people. It's about black experiences that whites don't appreciate. So maybe blacks *should* get special consideration. It evens things out."

What sorts of experiences will whites not appreciate? "Take the basketball thing. How would you like it if you learned that no matter how hard you worked and how well you did, there was going to be a group of people at the end who told you 'No, you can't' just because you were black?" She takes a deep breath. "Would you learn to work hard?" She suspects she got a break in getting admitted to Stanford, but feels that as a black woman bucking a history of exclusion, pockets of prejudice, and a system filled with white authorities who, while perhaps not malicious, are disposed to insensitivity, she deserved it. Thus she supports affirmative-action programs and thinks that Stanford should institute minority-admissions quotas, although she is not as dogmatic about it as many others. "The quotas should be flexible—they should depend on the number of qualified applicants you can find. Only people who are qualified should get into Stanford." She believes that the University should uphold all of its academic standards and only allow truly capable applicants to enter. "If you get a bunch of black students who show up and get D's and F's, then you haven't really done much good. But," she adds, "there aren't any unqualified blacks at Stanford." She supports the steps Stanford has taken to ensure minority inclusion in the revised Western Civilization courses and hopes for more minority faculty soon. If the number of blacks with Ph.D.s is small, as she hears it is, "then we should be doing something to get more blacks into college and graduate school."

Generally speaking, Anne believes there is considerable skepticism on campus about the academic qualifications of minority students. Her hunch is that many professors have doubts about her own abilities. However, she does not think they necessarily penalize her in the classroom, at least not in her experience. In fact, she notes that some professors will bend over backwards to help a black student who they feel is struggling in the course. "They will make extreme exceptions for you if you're black," she maintains. "I think they grade you easier on your papers. I did really poorly on this one physics midterm," she recalls. "I went to see the professor about it. He was really easy with me and said, 'No problem. Don't worry about it.' He said he would drop it off of my quarter grade and that it wouldn't even count, which was against his own rules. Right after I went in, this white student went in to ask him if he would drop his midterm grade because he did really bad too. The professor said, 'No way.'" She observes very candidly that she has learned the hard way, beginning with her experiences with racism while growing up, that many people cannot see past her skin color. "That sometimes works to my advantage, like with this professor," she says. "It's with me wherever I go, and I just take the results, good and bad, as they come."

Anne has given a lot of thought to the problem of racism, and makes a point of differentiating her views from those of the most influential black leaders on campus. "Racism is when one person hates another just because of their skin color. I don't see it only when the person in power is racist. I see it when anybody is prejudiced toward someone else. Many of the blacks here say that only whites can be racist because only they have the power. But that's simply not true," she says, insisting that racism is a "hateful attitude which anybody, black or white, can use against another person because of their skin color." If the extent to which one may act on one's hatred is limited by one's social power, it is hatred nonetheless—in Anne's own words, "a very hurtful evil." She puts it very simply: "I say that if you treat someone poorly because of their skin color, you're a racist no matter what your own skin color is or whether or not you have power."

By separating herself at all from any part of the black community at Stanford, Anne has incurred important social costs. A particularly sensitive issue is the pressure she feels from other blacks to subscribe to "black" ideas and values. She speaks of an accepted "line" and how various social problems should be diagnosed. "At the beginning of the year, black people who hadn't been around a lot of blacks were feeling insecure," she complains, "because they—the 'real' blacks—can make you feel like you're not black enough. Easily. There are always people around who are 'blacker than thou', you know?" Speech patterns, humor, dress, politics—she agrees that these are all aspects of the black culture. And she embraces any number of the informal black codes and restrictions that operate within the black community, except for one. She strongly resents black upperclass–men questioning "my black identity" or being told that an integral part of being 'black' involves associating exclusively with black people. "That's offensive to me," she says with an edge in her voice. "Everybody likes to be around people who are like them, but when you insist on being exclusive and won't allow anyone in because of the color of their skin, that's racist. I'm sorry, but it just is."

In Anne's opinion, self-segregation is central to the way the black community defines itself on campus. "I've gone to presentations on it in Ujamaa and listened to many discussions. A great many blacks feel very, very strongly about who they should associate with." She remembers one discussion in which the subject was interracial dating. She grimaces when she brings it up. "The workshop wasn't so bad—people talking about the purity of the black family. But then it becomes this big thing of not encouraging interaction with white students. Some friends of mine in Ujamaa went to some sorority parties and started hanging around with white guys—and they sure got the treatment," she says, shaking her head. "The upperclass women wouldn't even talk to them. It makes me mad that when black and white students are with each other and having a good time together, some blacks will always accuse the black students of selling out. You've got to be careful who you hang around with."

Or at least Anne feels she has to be careful *where* she spends time with whites. "You know, I've noticed that most of my white friends are not on this side of campus. I have to get out of Ujamaa to hang out with whites. Otherwise I get watched. I have to go to another dorm, or some other place away from where I live, to be social or my friends will think I'm trying to avoid them. I'm not the only one either," she says. "I think some of the younger black students hang out more on the other side of campus just because they can be at ease. Hell, I catch looks if I just get seen with whites in Tressider Union." There are times when she gets angry. She spent years getting abused because she was black, she says. "I learned to dislike people who let skin color prejudice them. Now I get here, and I'm supposed to not relate to whites because of their color? That's crazy. Like I said, I dislike prejudiced people whoever and wherever they are."

Anne is not at all in doubt about the importance of having a solid core of black friends at Stanford—not, however, to prove to them that she is black, but because she knows there will be times when someone is going to do or say something to try to make her feel bad or uncomfortable for being black. And no matter how many white friends she has and how close she may feel to them, she knows she will need to reach out to those who have felt the same pain. "Only we really know how much it hurts," she says quietly. Always practical, she understands, too, that she has to be able to meet and get along with as many people as she can on a campus like Stanford. "If there's a black culture here, there's also a white culture," she explains. "You have to learn to function in both. I didn't come here expecting to be surrounded by black students and black faculty. Sure, my cultural heritage is important to me, very important. But I'm not going to isolate myself. I think Stanford has a lot to offer me. That's why I came here," she stresses. "And so I know that if I'm going to have a chance at success in what I do with my life in the world out there, I'm going to have to make it here first."

If there are occasions when she gets upset, there are also times, she admits, when she is not sure what she thinks. "I don't know what I feel sometimes. I just do what I believe is right." What she considers "right" is her commitment to the struggle against racism in any form. Consequently, she feels the Black Student Union plays an important role on campus. "I guess white students think the BSU 'always wants something'"—she emphasizes each word—"but it has to be vocal. I think it's healthy when you bring out into the open different ideas and all the differences the groups on campus have. You come up with some kind of healthy discussion." She works with the Black Recruitment and Orientation Committee that serves black students who are either considering coming to Stanford or are newly enrolled, hoping to ease the transition to the University for blacks who have known only majority black environments. It is a program she cares deeply about. Yet she acknowledges that it often causes her personal discomfort. "It's like I get it from both sides," she says. "There are whites who are plain prejudiced and others who are patronizing. Then there are blacks who are prejudiced toward whites and tell me I'm going to be in trouble with them if I don't feel the same way." She stops for a moment and stares off into space. "I think about it a lot, what it means to be black here. Sometimes I find it hard to fit in anywhere on campus," she says, managing a smile that barely masks her disappointment. One way or another, her blackness has forced her into a social limbo, regarded with suspicion by two camps for very different reasons.

From everything she has seen and heard since coming to Stanford, Anne thinks racism is a "very serious campus issue." But her views are not ethnically bound, principally because she has developed an acute intolerance for anyone of any race who "feels hostility towards someone because of their color." Yet she "suspects" there lurks at Stanford some form of racism, "although I'm not sure I can really define it," which may have more to do with her past experiences with racism and discrimination than with any personal exposure to racist policies or practices at Stanford. "I've never been the victim of racist harassment or any sort of intimidation since I've been here," she says. "But I realize that some whites are just uncomfortable around black people. I think that's unfortunate. Most white students haven't spent a lot of time with blacks, so they really don't know us, not as individuals, I mean. But that doesn't mean they're racists, does it?" She believes all students should be required to take an ethnic-studies course before they graduate so that they can become more knowledgeable about different cultures, including minority students "who should study people who aren't of their own ethnic group." Racial barriers are best broken down, she says, when people of different backgrounds work together on matters they have in common. "A lot of racism exists because people don't understand one another. I think we're all hurt by cultural ignorance. That's why I don't like to see blacks separating themselves from whites in the dining room or anywhere else on campus—and I wish white students would make more of an effort to mix when they see this kind of separatism," she adds.

Anne reaches into her shoulder bag resting on a chair and pulls out a copy of the *Stanford Daily*, the student newspaper. She is upset with a column written by a black student who has claimed that black people at Stanford regularly come under attack and that every day she gets the same clear message: "Go back where you came from, you do not belong here." Anne tosses the paper aside. "That's not the message I get at all," she says. "Sure, there are racial problems and there've been some bad incidents, but that's not the true picture of Stanford. This used to be a place for whites only, and not very long ago. But the campus has been changing pretty fast. My class—it's something like 40 percent minorities, isn't it? That's what I see. I think the real story is that with so many people from different backgrounds thrown together, we all get along pretty well." She puts the *Daily* back in her bag. "The real news about Stanford is what a black friend of mine said. It's like a small town, with our own problems and personality. But we're lucky to be able to see our faults, to talk about them openly, and move on."

III.
The Frustrated White

It is easy to see why the Stanford life-style agrees with "Ted." Although born and raised in the Northwest, he has grown accustomed to the California way of doing things. He is a die-hard frisbee player, never misses a chance to play softball, and spends long afternoons on spacious Roble Field in shorts and sports goggles. He is soft-spoken, quiet, and thoughtful, yet quite comfortable in social settings. He is active in dorm government and a central figure at dorm recreational events. During the lazy, sunny days of the spring quarter, he prefers to study outdoors, working on his tan. "Well, actually I never really tan," he admits. "For me it's more like sunburn, peel, sunburn, peel." He takes his studies as seriously as he takes his recreation. Majoring in math science, he maintains a 3.9 GPA. "Most of the time I like my work," he states. "What can I say?"

Ted's father works as an engineer and supports the family comfortably in their suburban home. In Ted's neighborhood there were few minorities, but the student body in his high school included about 20 percent minorities. Nevertheless, his interaction with blacks before coming to Stanford was limited. The University offers him his first real environment for interracial relationships, an opportunity for which he is thankful. What personal experience he had with blacks and other minorities in high school, he feels, did not prepare him for the challenges of race relations at Stanford.

One lesson he does consider valuable involved an incident in his home town, one with which he had no direct connection. "There was a black teenage girl who claimed she had been harassed by some white guys. She eventually charged that they had sexually threatened her, and there was this big controversy," he says. "There were protests over racism and the whole bit."

A few months later it was discovered that the young woman had fabricated a scenario in which the white men had allegedly tormented her. "I don't know what the whole story behind it was, but I did learn just how explosive racial stuff can be. It's a high-emotion thing, and you've got to be careful."

Around the dorm, Ted is known as someone who speaks his mind and says what he means. He lives in the dormitory adjacent to Ujamaa. One of the freshmen who defaced the Ujamaa Beethoven poster with Negro features lived in Ted's dorm, and almost immediately after the incident Ted took a leading role in trying to secure what he felt would be a just outcome for all of the parties involved. His efforts brought nothing but personal frustration.

Ted's initial concerns arose from the reporting that appeared in the student *Daily*. He went to a meeting between residents of Ujamaa and his dorm to discuss the allegedly racist incident, but quickly discovered that everyone in the room was visibly angry. The meeting ended in shouting and crying. Realizing that the potential fallout across the campus could be intense, he went to the student newspaper with firsthand details of the meeting in an effort to ensure that what had occurred would be reported accurately and with as little hype as possible. "I was the first person to get there. I told what had happened, and they said 'Great.' Later, some of the black leaders went with a different version. Guess which account they printed? Not mine," he says, not hiding the unhappiness he still feels. "They made it sound like this huge race riot. That was the beginning of the explosion."

Later, the University's Office of Residential Education came up with a solution, then reneged on its own announced position, and finally suggested another. Once again Ted stepped in to offer his ideas. "Residential Education first said that we [the dorms] should handle the problem ourselves. Then, when the black leaders didn't like that, Res Ed totally changed their tune," he says. "It went from us having to educate them [the offenders] in racial sensitivity one day, to expelling them from the dorm complex and forbidding them to even return the next."

His indignation was shared by many of his dormmates. "We have a small dorm, and everyone was worried about our friend charged with committing this racist act. We felt like we were totally subject to whatever the black leadership in Ujamaa wanted. If anybody disagreed with them, they were *automatically* a racist, you know?" Determined to do something, Ted decided on two courses of action. First, he and some friends wrote a letter to the *Daily* expressing their displeasure with the behavior of Residential Education. Second, he went to see the residential dean in charge of the west side of campus. "He was basically a jerk concerned with covering his butt," he states with a deep sigh. "He made a comment to the effect that the two freshmen were going to have to be punished because a lot of people from his office had worked hard on handling the complaints from the black community. Can you believe that? He actually said this to me— like it really didn't matter if they were treated fairly, just so *his* life was easier and people would stop being mad at Res Ed."

Ted also thinks the University went to great lengths to cover up some of the anti-white backlash that followed the events in Ujamaa. Around his dorm, he says, it is common knowledge that after the incident several pictures of white students were vandalized in Ujamaa, and that some members of the black community circulated anti-white flyers and buttons. Residential officials asked white students in Ujamaa not to take the story to the *Daily*, promising to handle the backlash officially. "But not a damn thing was ever done," Ted reports, with more than a hint of irritation in his voice. "They didn't care about inflaming the incident when it was against the white freshmen," he charges. "That was racist. The people in the administration are so scared of being called racist they're afraid to tell it like it is. Even the fact-finding account the University published in the *Daily* played down the black reaction. That's total bullshit!"

Ted's criticism of the way the Ujamaa matter was handled was, at least in part, the result of having been caught up in events that affected him more deeply and personally than he ever could have imagined possible. But the rancor with which he reacted against the developments that followed the racial incident may also have had its roots in an experience that predates the campus controversy. Soon after Ted came to Stanford as a freshman, he began dating a freshman woman he met at a party. They had not been going out together for very long, but he felt comfortable in the relationship. "We got along really well, and had a lot of the same interests. We both liked sports, liked the same movies, that sort of thing. We were good friends," he says. However, the woman was black, and while at first that caused no immediate problems for either of them, her friends in the black community began pressuring her to give up the relationship. "It got kind of bad. When certain friends were around, she'd feel uptight in even talking to me. Eventually the relationship just crumbled, not so much because she caved in and refused to see me," he observes, "but because she couldn't continue to see me and still be comfortable with it. She took a lot of criticism, which really bothered her. The pressure just got to be too much."

Perhaps as a result of this episode, or perhaps in spite of it, Ted has made repeated efforts throughout his years at Stanford to increase his understanding of interracial relationships and, in particular, the differences in the various minority cultures on campus. "I did not expect racism to be a major issue at Stanford, but when I got here the whole topic just sort of confronted me. I think that happens to most white students," he explains. Beginning in his freshman year, he took deliberate steps toward creating interracial ties. He attended dorm discussions and campus forums on the race situation, kept abreast of the debates and grievances in the minority communities, and availed himself of many of the cultural educational programs sponsored by campus ethnic groups. Because his efforts have been intentional and marked by such firm determination, and since his own education in these matters started with a personal appreciation of some of the obvious barriers to interracial relations, he weathers his setbacks with a certain aplomb. For example, he tells of the time his freshman roommate was rushing a fraternity. "We were sitting at a table with a few black guys and the conversation turned to white fraternities. One of the black guys said how racist the frats were—how they were anti-black. Then he started really criticizing the fraternity my roommate was rushing, saying that they wouldn't let any black guys in, and that anyone involved in that frat was obviously a racist.

"That was too much for my roommate," Ted recalls with unabashed sympathy. "He quickly informed the black students— this really rattled them, too—that the rush director for his fraternity happened to be a black man. Then he got up and stormed away from the table. He was steaming. I mean, we were both tired of being made to feel like we were racists. Why should we have to take that crap? That particular conversation was just the last straw for my roommate," Ted states, the incident as fresh in his mind as if it had taken place yesterday. "I stayed around and tried to talk it out awhile, but things were just too tense." He shakes his head and, in a gesture of frustration, swipes at his shoes. "Hell, you've just got to forget it and try again later. You can't just walk away or you go on being angry."

But things have not always been so intensely unpleasant. Whether because of his interest in the history and culture of the diverse groups that comprise the campus community today or his natural inclination to being social and amicable, Ted counts as many if not more minorities in his circle of close friends than whites. He currently rooms with a minority student. Off campus, he has involved himself in a tutoring program for elementary-school children in East Palo Alto, a low-income, chiefly black community not far from the University. "It's totally true that minorities are worse off economically," he notes, "and I'm trying not to be part of the problem." His efforts, he believes, have produced positive results, "at least with respect to my personal understanding of what it's like to be a minority student here." First, he has an increased awareness of issues that lead to racial tension. "I have greater sensitivity to racism now and how it could be going on even if I wouldn't necessarily know it. Everything isn't always out in the open. There's a lot of stuff that goes on beneath the surface." He has also learned to guard against his own prejudices. "Racism," he explains, "can be sort of subconscious. I mean we often go by what we're told. I think I sometimes have fears about blacks—like when I'm walking alone somewhere and I see a black coming toward me. I'm more likely to suspect them of being a criminal. Is that racism? I don't know. All I know is that I don't feel that way about Asians or Chicanos."

The expression on Ted's face is sober, almost stern. Taking a deep breath, he continues more slowly and carefully. "Look, it's not like I don't know there are real problems between blacks and whites. But I'm tired of being lumped together with racists and racist history because of my skin color. I'm white, but I'm *not* part of the problem." His early interactions with black students on campus have led him to a cautious appraisal of Stanford's black community. "Some blacks isolate themselves from the white community. I think they feel more uncomfortable with white people. And there's that pressure from the black community to hang out with blacks. I don't think that's right at all. It goes against everything we should be working for, like breaking down antagonisms and getting to know each other as human beings." He shakes his head in disapproval. "I think the segregation that occurs on campus is largely the minority groups separating themselves."

He draws attention to a division in the black community between those blacks who do not associate with whites and those who do. In his view, a smaller but significant segment of the black community—"many of the most activist black students, for example"—choose to segregate. "Some blacks are OK to hang out with. But others kind of give you the feeling, 'Don't come around me if you're white.' The BSU really concentrates on the differences between whites and blacks, and that tends to make them separate. Just highlighting the differences makes cooperation harder and leads to isolation. They could concentrate on what we have in common too. I'm all for cultural diversity, but I don't think that should mean segregation. Anyway, I don't think there are a lot of black students out there that wholeheartedly agree with the BSU."

Ted's biggest complaint is that, based on what he has observed, the black students who are the most outspoken in calling for an appreciation of cultural differences and the education of whites in ethnic sensitivity are the least likely to relate to whites on a sociable basis. Therefore he bitterly resents accusations that white students at Stanford are excluding blacks from mainstream social arenas. "There were these two black guys in my dorm last year. They were never around. The only time they showed up was for our dorm talk on racism—racial harmony. I mean come on! They talk about racial harmony but they were never there!" When Ted thinks about the issue of racism on campus, his reflex is to consider it in interpersonal rather than institutional terms. What good is education in racial sensitivity, he asks, if whites and blacks are not both encouraged and willing to interact freely with one another? "It's like they want my respect, and sometimes my help," he says, "but that we can't be friends, you know?" That is the starting place of Ted's frustration and discouragement with race relations at Stanford—the perception of a doctrine of "inclusion with separation" in a part of the black student community. He quips half-seriously, "Hey, didn't the Supreme Court already rule that separate but equal isn't constitutional? I thought that's what the *Brown* decision back in the 1950s was supposed to have settled once and for all."

However, he is not indifferent to many of the concerns of the blacks and, in fact, supports most of the demands that make up the "minority agenda." He backs fully the call for inclusion of "multicultural education" in the required University curriculum on the grounds that "students need to know about people who are culturally different from the white majority," and approves of the sweeping changes in Stanford's much-touted Western Culture program. He agrees that there should be a greater number of minority faculty members as well as minority counselors and deans, and supports an increased emphasis on ethnic studies generally as a way of ensuring that the distinct cultures of minorities are not excluded. "I think most students want to see courses relating to women and minorities, Third World cultures, that sort of thing," he says. "I'm all for anything that will help stop the separatism and polarizing on campus, and that's why, I guess, I think a broad education is our best hope."

But Ted draws the line at the more aggressive affirmative-action policies. "The different backgrounds of people should be considered when they apply to college," he maintains. "If their background includes having been subjected to racial prejudice and discrimination, then that should be taken into account. But just the fact that their skin is a particular color—I don't think that's particularly relevant." It bothers him that special advantages in the admissions process at Stanford are given to black students who may not even need to be treated in a preferential way. "Why the heck are they giving affirmative-action credits to a black when in fact he may have grown up middle-class and in the suburbs?" he wants to know. "At my high school," he remembers, "the counselor told the students to really emphasize any ethnic heritage they had in filling out the college applications because it would make it easier to get in. I felt left out. I know that's really stupid, but it was a tense time for me." The general feeling was, he says, that if the student were a reasonably qualified minority, he or she had a "lock" on getting into the college of his or her choice. "My best friend, who had a 4.0 GPA and great SAT scores, didn't make it to Stanford or to the Eastern schools," Ted states. "This black kid at school did. He wasn't disadvantaged—his parents were richer than mine—and he didn't even make the top 10 percent of our graduating class. It's a victory for blacks, and I'm glad for that, but it was depressing for my friend and me."

It is not surprising that he strongly disapproves of the idea of minimum minority quotas and enforced proportional representation in Stanford's student body. "Racism," he points out, "is when someone is denied an opportunity because of their race. Just because everybody isn't equal in achievement doesn't mean there's racism. I can't play football the way those guys on the team do, and I sure as heck can't sing the way I'd like to. But that's because I don't have the talent, not those talents anyway. It sure has nothing to do with racism." He tries to be sensitive to the difficulties and challenges facing blacks in our society, but he dismisses blanket charges of racism against the University. "I'm not sure I understand the term 'institutional racism'," he admits, "but I don't see how Stanford is a racist institution." He pauses, visibly aggravated, and then continues: "If anything, I think the University bends over backwards to be accommodating. Maybe we're not totally there yet, but I don't see how anyone can say the University isn't cooperating with the black community."

Ted considers himself someone who has taken a determined interest in improving his understanding of black, Asian-American and other minority students at Stanford. He has made a strong effort to "relate better," as he puts it, firmly believing that developing relationships with "people who are different from me" is the key to reducing racial tensions on campus. He is terribly frustrated by the reluctance of some blacks to interact with him at all, much less establish a friendship that could persist long after graduation. When he has pursued reconciliation, as in the aftermath of the Ujamaa incident, he has met with what he feels is defensive and shallow University policy-making. "I see the administration investing great energy in staying politically correct, while spending very little time or effort in creative problem-solving or providing decisive leadership," he says. Having made attempts to improve race relations in his own spheres of social activity and influence, he feels somewhat betrayed by the outcomes. In spite of his overtures, he is gloomy about the immediate prospects of lessening interracial strife on campus. "Sometimes my dormmates and I try to initiate something with the black community in Ujamaa, but we just can't get anything off the ground. They don't want anything to do with us. And it's like if any of the blacks relate to us, they're in trouble with other blacks. So we kind of live here, and they live there, and there's this wall."

Between Power and Integration: Dilemmas of Race and Racism

During the last two decades, Americans have had more than their national share of being victimized by language. It is as if words and slogans have become our tyrannical masters rather than instruments to help assess and fulfill our democratic goals. In the 1960s, for example, an unthinking tyranny of terms took a known and once-respected word such as "relevance" and converted it into its opposite. As invoked in its polemical heyday, it bullied the opposition instead of persuading it. Who, after all, wanted to be known as an *opponent* of relevance? Didn't opposing relevance make one an exponent of irrelevance? It soon became an embarrassing cliche and was pretty much lost to respectable discourse.

"Racism" has had something of the same history in recent years. Many of those who use the terms "racism" or "racist" use them in so many different and imprecise ways that they have almost been robbed of any meaning at all. Too often "racist" is simply wielded as a harsh accusation, as if verbal abuse were a substitute for thought and analysis. One remembers when (now Senator) Daniel P. Moynihan, in 1965, drew attention to the deterioration of the black family. He cited (among other things) the connection between the curve of unemployment and that of family dissolution, and the new correlation between family instability and welfare dependency. He was immediately attacked as a racist—and although what he said over 25 years ago is now pretty much conventional wisdom, in some quarters such analyses are still attacked as just one more racist slander on the black family.

There are those who charge that whites who oppose busing as the primary remedy for school desegregation are blocking efforts to achieve racial equality and are hostile to blacks (which may strike the many black parents who are also against busing as less than convincing). They disregard the possibility of another explanation—that both blacks and whites might honestly oppose the imposition of busing to bring about racial balance in the schools because they think it threatens the personal well-being and academic achievement of their children. And why should whites who have long recognized that blacks in this country have suffered from pernicious discrimination—and who *support* compensatory government programs that will assist blacks in acquiring training and education skills—now be regarded as "symbolic racists" who, in their support of such traditional American values as hard work, personal effort, and individual accomplishment, are actually providing a cover for their more deeply felt prejudice and racial hostility?[1] Clearly there are many people who openly vent their hatred of blacks and other minorities and regularly oppose all efforts to grant them equal rights. But does it follow, as many have charged, that because many whites are dissatisfied with certain high-cost government programs or policies that they feel have proven to be ineffective—and that they would just as strongly oppose if such programs were intended to help whites—they are therefore opposed to racial equality and, by extension, are racists either of the old "redneck" variety or the new symbolic kind?

The real question is how many of our problems should be seen or defined only in terms of racism. For example, many educators have long insisted that it is not racist to require ghetto students to learn standard English, thereby treating them as the equals of the great majority of students. Black children are already weighted down with enough handicaps in our society. For many years men and women from all walks of life have been deeply concerned about the special ills that trap millions of black Americans in failure and despair. But are they promoting racism if they suggest that high rates of unemployment, illiteracy, drugs, alcohol, AIDS cases and violent crime have not been imposed upon the black underclass by white society or cannot simply be attributed to covert white discrimination? The significant disparities in academic performance between black and white students remain an urgent problem. But isn't it a crude oversimplification to cite racism or discrimination as the reason that blacks generally have below-average grades and a high dropout rate? And does racism account for the wide difference between whites' and blacks' SAT scores and other test results, especially when other minorities that have also suffered from ugly discrimination in our society do so well?

It would be foolish to think that racism no longer exists— foolish and untrue. Yet it has been used so often to explain almost everything that other factors that could contribute to a deeper understanding of existing problems are ignored. One of the reasons it is not always easy to determine the nature and extent of racism on college campuses is that many of the reported incidents that have been described as "racist" do not follow a similar pattern and are therefore open to questions of fact and interpretation. Racist leaflets ("Get your black asses back to Africa") and threats ("Death Nigger" scratched on a black academic counselor's office door) are clearly evidence of racist thinking and behavior. But should the same be said of the slogan "Equal rights, not special rights" that has appeared on some campuses?

There is strong opposition to programs that take the form of race-based preferential treatment because they are believed to violate principles of equality. Such opposition may be considered right or wrong, fair or unfair. But is it evidence of racism? When Ira Michael Heyman was Chancellor of the University of California at Berkeley, he acknowledged that there had been few racist incidents on campus. But he was not discounting their importance, he said. "I perceive them to fit into the larger framework of the general mood in the United States that includes the blunting of affirmative-action programs." Does this mean that Heyman equates racism with opposition to affirmative action, or that such opposition is, in fact, racist?[2]

"Racism" and "racist" are not words that should be bandied about recklessly. Although a significant number of black students at Stanford (and elsewhere) maintain that racism is inherent in the "white power structure" that dominates the campus, most white students, as well as many blacks, think of racism as it is commonly understood by Americans generally—namely, discrimination against individuals and groups because of their background or membership in one race or another. Hitler's persecution of the Jews and his perverse ideas about Aryan supremacy was racism at its worst. It is also racism when an individual is denied all the rights of democratic citizenship on the basis of color or national origin, or when someone is advantaged or disadvantaged for no other or better reason than the particular racial group to which he or she belongs. Long before they get to college, more and more of today's students learn that racism deals in stereotypes. Someone who does not judge people who are black or white, brown or yellow, Jewish or Catholic, according to their individual qualities, but simply lumps them all together into categories like "foreigners," is a racist in the making. Weekend golfers who tell disparaging "jokes" or "funny" stories about blacks or Jews that they would not tell in front of a black or a Jew are spreading the virus of racism and prejudice. In recognizing that skin color or national origin is irrelevant to what makes a person a brilliant musician or a first-rate athlete, many of the Stanford students who were interviewed made the point that "real people" are not stereotypes—which is one reason several of them took exception to the statement of the Black Student Union chairman who said, "I do not like most white people." It sounded to them like something a white racist and bigot would say about black people.

One of the principal issues that has been at the center of the debate about the role of race and ethnicity at Stanford is the movement toward "multicultural education," which, as the *Washington Post* has observed, has become the all-purpose educational buzzword of the 1990s. The argument is a passionate one, led by those who attack the traditional emphasis in schools and colleges on American history and Western civilization as "Eurocentric." The question of how and whether to reform the curriculum in Western Culture was debated for almost a year on the Stanford campus, resulting in a retitling of the required one-year course to "Culture, Ideas, Values" (with "Western" removed).[3] If the only concerns were how best to provide students with new and constructive information on the historical roles played by women or by blacks and other minority groups in America, and what measures to take to enrich our undergraduates' understanding and appreciation of talented nonwhite or non-male writers and artists from other continents and cultures, the dispute would be short-lived and quite easily resolved. After all, faculties are continually adding new courses and revising core curriculums along pedagogical lines to reflect the expansion of knowledge in a rapidly changing world. Furthermore, in the personal interviews with Stanford undergraduates, almost three-quarters of the white students and close to 90 percent of the blacks agreed with the recommendation that studies of other cultures, including ethnic studies in particular, should in some way be a graduation requirement.

But the debate is not solely about the importance of including in the curriculum opportunities for students to study other cultures in the world and to learn from them. The issue is filled with such emotion and intensity because many of the critics of Western civilization have charged that African-Americans, Asian-Americans, Puerto Ricans, Latinos, and Native Americans are "victims of an intellectual and educational oppression that has characterized the culture and institutions of the United States and the European American world for centuries." In emphasizing the University's "systematic bias" toward Western culture, a black student said, "Look at the Stanford curriculum and what do you find? First, white control. Second, white control. Third, more of the same. And what the courses in American history teach everyone who isn't white is that we're supposed to rejoice in this great melting pot, while our own history of subjugation is ignored as if we didn't have any roots worth knowing about. And people wonder why we say that the Eurocentric curricula doesn't mean much to African-Americans and Indians and Hispanics and the other groups that have been oppressed," he added sternly. Echoing a sentiment expressed by a number of other black students at Stanford, he said that every time he is told about the great contributions of the Founding Fathers, "I say to myself, 'They are not my Fathers.' I don't see any black faces around the table where the Constitution was drafted."

And then he returned to his central theme. "There's a lot of talk about adding to the curriculum—women's studies, black studies, making sure the textbooks are rewritten so minority students can see who they are, develop some self-esteem, that sort of thing. And that's all fine. But the issue is not whether we should add courses to the curriculum. The real question is whose history is going to be taught and who's going to teach it. What's really at stake is what's always at stake—power. Who's going to be in charge?"

However, a serious problem arises whenever students (or any other groups) are convinced that complex academic issues can be easily reduced to questions of power. For example, should the college curriculum be treated as if it were akin to the way a big-city mayor hands out favors and rewards to constituency groups? To accept such a proposition, much less put it into practice, is to believe that in the name of "multiculturalism," the faculty should evaluate the demands of different ethnic groups on campus—specifically, the demand that *their* histories be more heavily weighted—by estimating which group has the most power. It is also to deny what many professors at Stanford (and elsewhere) would claim is not deniable—that Europe has had the largest influence on this nation's values and institutions and that the democratic tradition (which happens to have been European) has given the world the principles and ideals of individual freedom, self-criticism through open and vigorous debate, and, perhaps most distinctive in our heritage, protest and dissent.[4]

A black student at Stanford—a moderate by his own definition (and not a member of the Black Student Union)—said that while he had much to complain about in contemporary American society, "I have taken courses here—courses that are called 'Eurocentric' by many students—that taught me about my own past history in this country, about some of the imperialist wars the United States has fought, about some of the terrible treatment Catholics and Jews and the Chinese have experienced as

Americans. I've learned all these things because a great part of our Western system of education has involved the right to look at the good and the bad about ourselves. How many other cultures in the world can make that claim?" He could easily have pointed to the Chinese students during the 1989 Tianenmen Square uprising who raised the Statue of Liberty and quoted Montesquieu, Jefferson, and Locke. Or he could have recalled that W.E.B. Dubois, the African-American intellectual and political leader, did not believe that Western culture had meaning and importance only to a limited group of white Europeans and Americans. At the turn of the century in a Jim Crow America, Dubois wrote:

> I sit with Shakespeare and he winces not.
> Across the color line I walk arm in arm with
> Balzac and Dumas, where smiling men and
> welcoming women glide in gilded halls. From
> out of the caves of evening that swing between
> the strong-limbed earth and the tracery of the
> stars, I summon Aristotle and Aurelius and what
> soul I will, and they come all graciously with
> no scorn or condescension. So, wed with Truth,
> I dwell above the evil.

Thus the central issue is sharply defined: Should Western culture, and, in particular, the educational tradition it has produced, be looked upon as fundamentally a struggle of class against class, group against group, and, most especially, victim against oppressor? Or is a primary lesson of Western culture and American history that the essential themes of freedom and political democracy transcend lines of race, class, and ancestry? When Dean of Yale College, Donald Kagan, spoke to the freshman class of 1990, he ended by telling them to "take pride in your family and the culture your forebears have brought. Learn as much as you can . . . of what the cultures of others have to offer.

But do not let our separate heritages draw us apart."

The concern about students on our campuses "drawing apart" has raised other questions about "multiculturalism." Will black students get the education they need only if they study themselves and their culture? Will the academic performance of black students, whether in high school or in college, be improved by making the curriculum more African-centered? And closely tied to these concerns is the question whether books and ideas themselves should be connected to the race of their authors or to those who make use of them. It is one thing for most Stanford undergraduates to agree that more classes in African-American studies are needed, in the same sense that they favor more minority faculty members. But it is something very different to argue that African-American professors must teach the classes. There is general agreement that one should include the works of men or women or minorities in a course on the history of thought because of the significant ideas that underlie them, but not simply because they were written by men or women or minorities. In determining which ideas (or "great books") have been important and influential, one must begin with an eye to how they began, what trajectory they have traveled, and why they have made their way from the past to the present. As the writer and author Max Lerner has observed, every great change in history comes about through the rise and fall of ideas. But to label an idea as "white" or "black" or "male" or "female" is to violate and degrade it.

For many black students at Stanford, the debate over the meaning and direction of "multiculturalism" is closely tied to one of their fundamental concerns—namely, whether the new rush to "diversity"—the word has become one of the shibboleths of the 1990s on college campuses across the country—will turn into what a black student activist called "another case of white manipulation of African-Americans. 'Diversity' sounds good," he said, "but who's going to decide what's in it for us—the white administrators? Is the white faculty going to tell me what a college education means for me, or am I going to have something to say about it?" He had put his finger on a matter of increasing controversy, underscoring the fact that the "celebration of diversity" does not, in fact, rest on a core of basic values and assumptions shared by every group on campus. Writing in *The New York Times* as "liberal whites," two Columbia University students who felt they shared many of the demands voiced by black students, such as more minority students to be admitted to our universities, more black tenured professors, and more emphasis on African-American studies, said they also felt that "we have no place in what appears to be today's black movement. Our experience has led us to realize that our black classmates are not simply seeking integration into a white society. They want equality, true," they wrote, "but they do not want to see themselves defined by white society—they are not aspiring whites. They have their own culture and their own background, with its own character. They fiercely guard their prerogative to define that culture."

The University of California at Berkeley, which frequently holds up for public acclaim its newly achieved student diversity, points to the fact that no single ethnic or racial group constitutes a majority today. However, a sixteen-month report on racial attitudes called the "Diversity Project" (made public in 1990) revealed that there is far less mingling of cultures on the campus than its ethnic and racial diversity might suggest. It stated that many students find themselves divided by racial and ethnic barriers that have fostered suspicions and created misunderstandings about those on the other side. Blacks, Hispanics, and Asian-Americans get tracked into segregated student life for reasons that include pressures from their own groups. Study sessions and parties, as well as student political, social, and professional groups, tend to splinter along racial and ethnic lines. Groups like the Black Sociology Student Association and gatherings like all-Asian dances serve as a source of strength for minority students, but are also obstacles to cross-racial relationships. As a result, the campus is Balkanized, according to the 23 UC-Berkeley social scientists who conducted the interview-study of 230 students. Many students, especially those who said they came to Berkeley in search of diversity, expressed dismay about the way everything from sitting in a cafeteria to chatting between classes takes on a racial tone. "All students have to figure out whom they are going to hang out with, but on this campus it becomes a racial question," the report observed.[5]

As we saw earlier, these very same concerns surfaced time and again in the personal interviews with Stanford students, especially among white undergraduates who lamented the fact that although those who promoted cultural diversity talked in terms of inclusion, the political reality was that what was practiced on campus had very little to do with either inclusion or diversity. Furthermore, the racial divisions described in the Berkeley report reflect what is happening today on most of the leading campuses in the country. According to a national survey issued in early 1990 by the Carnegie Foundation, "Students are increasingly separating themselves in unhealthy ways." Gone is any idea of the melting pot, which for many white students had been something they had pretty much always believed in, if only in a vague yet positive way. Now they are being told that racial and ethnic enclaves enable minority students to discover or renew a sense of group identity and pride in what the Berkeley report calls "havens in a heartless world" that, in the words of Prof. Troy Duster, the project director, "harden like rocks in the first six months."

Project researchers also found that much of the campus tension stemmed from an intensely competitive admissions process. Over the last ten years, Berkeley has radically changed the way in which its undergraduates are selected. As part of the process of diversifying the student body, white-freshman enrollment in 1989 and 1990 was only about 33 percent (the total percentage of white students at Berkeley in 1980 was 66 percent), while Hispanic and Asian-American enrollments in 1990 were 22 and 30 percent, respectively. Black enrollment has dropped to about 8 percent, reflecting a national and statewide downward trend. According to the report, stories abound of black, American Indian, or Hispanic students "stealing" admissions spots from Asian or white students who scored higher on an academic index. And minority students complained that no matter how hard they worked, they were not accepted as legitimate students by classmates. "I feel like I have 'Affirmative Action' stamped on my forehead," said one black student who was interviewed for the project.

Alarmed by the many pressures it found on Berkeley students to socialize and affiliate with "one's own kind," the faculty report proposed ways to ease tensions—by forming small multiracial groups of students to talk about their concerns, for example, and by having the faculty encourage students of different backgrounds to work together on projects of mutual interest. (Students interviewed for the Diversity Project said that the backdrops for their most rewarding experiences with people of other backgrounds were activities without a racial focus, such as sports teams, a band, or a choir.) Somewhat incongruously, however, white students were specifically encouraged to form groups "to rescue an ethnic heritage without risk or fear of the charge of racism." According to the report, "Jewish students, or Italian or Irish students with an easy trace to their ethnic backgrounds might find such affinities and recognize this as socially and politically acceptable." Precisely how the fostering of white ethnic groupings would lead to more friendships across ethnic lines and to new efforts to promote interracial harmony at Berkeley was not made clear. "I don't think it makes much sense," one faculty member was prompted to remark, "to look for ways to get black and other minority students to look beyond themselves and to reach outward to the whole campus community at the same time you are urging white students to look inward and to their own special groups to define themselves."[6]

The Berkeley report raised a number of different but related questions, among the most important of which is who decides when free speech and free inquiry should be banned to protect students and the rest of the campus community from "bad ideas," "offensive expressions," or "politically incorrect" views. The issue that has created the most controversy—and, on some campuses, deepened racial antagonisms—is that of racism and academic freedom or, more specifically, accusations of racism and racist speech and the commitment to defend unpopular views and ideas even when they are branded as racist. "White liberals talk all the time about fighting prejudice and discrimination," said a black Stanford student, "but when it comes to curbing racist speech that is insulting and degrading to people of color, they hide in the First Amendment. That's easy for them to do because they've never felt the pain of racist speech or racist posters or racist graffiti. Remember the Beethoven incident on this campus? To most white students that was only a free-speech issue, something to debate in class, maybe. Sure. They weren't the victims. We were, which is why it hurt."

But how does a university try to impose tolerance and civility on its students? In 1988, the University of Michigan's answer was to issue a sweeping prohibition on "any behavior, verbal or physical, that stigmatizes or victimizes an individual on the basis of race, ethnicity, religion, national origin, sex, sexual orientation, creed, ancestry, age, marital status, handicap, or Vietnam-era veteran status." A year later a U.S. District Court struck down the policy as unconstitutionally vague, but not before 146 Michigan students had been hauled up on charges. Nor has the "hate speech" code adopted in 1989 at the University of Wisconsin, under which nine students were disciplined for making derogatory remarks, fared any better. In October 1991, a federal district judge ruled that the code violated students'

First Amendment rights.

Officials at the University of Wisconsin had argued that their speech code was defensible under the "fighting words" doctrine established by the Supreme Court in 1942 (*Chaplinsky v. New York*). The Court ruled that words that "by their very utterance inflict injury or tend to incite an immediate breach of the peace" do not deserve constitutional protection. In the last several years a number of institutions—Stanford among them—have enacted codes or issued statements designed to penalize students who use racist, sexist, or homophobic slurs against others. At the University of California at Berkeley, "fighting words" are defined as "personally abusive epithets . . . likely to provide a violent reaction whether or not they actually do so . . . or create a hostile and intimidating environment which will interfere with the victim's ability to pursue effectively his or her education." Whether this version of the "fighting words" policy (and others like it) will pass constitutional muster may not be known until the Supreme Court rules in its current term on a Minnesota law that penalizes "hate crimes." Apart from the legal issues, however, the question of whether a policy aimed at barring offensive speech will serve to defend students of color against the reported upsurge of campus bigotry and "racist aggression," or will turn out to be a solution in search of a problem, is a matter of considerable debate. "University administrators are facing what they perceive to be a crisis of ethnic intolerance, and they're scrambling around for a response," a UC-Berkeley law professor commented. "The easiest thing when you don't know what to do is you take a stick and you hit. A lot of this has been part of a politics of race that is emerging at UC and in society in general," he observed. "'Racism' is a term that's thrown around campuses these days with abandon."[7]

To many black students, all the talk about the First Amendment and due process is seen as the "usual runaround we always get." Writing in the student *Daily*, a black senior at Stanford majoring in African and Afro-American studies said, "Here, where acts of clear racist harassment and intimidation have been turned into issues of free speech and de facto defenses of racists, black people get a clear message: 'Go back where you came from, you do not belong here.' I feel this message every day, even under all of Stanford's veils of pluralism and multicultural diversity." The message she wanted from Stanford was that "more funds must be committed to the financial aid of students of color over their entire undergraduate careers . . . and that any act of racism, sexism, or homophobia will not be tolerated." But an African-American studies major from UC-Berkeley, who supports the campus policy of suppressing "fighting words" that produce incidents of overt harassment, also maintained that the policy was "just a tool" minorities might use "to restructure the university." Restating the argument of militant blacks at Stanford, he said that the real issue is who has the power in the university. "It's going to be a matter of who owns this place, and whether we have the ability to really make a difference here." As for enforcing the "fighting words" policy, he further insisted that it be applied only to white students. "Racism is prejudice plus power," he said, "and people of color are powerless. There's no power behind calling somebody a honky, but there sure is power behind calling somebody a bitch, or a nigger or a spick."

Not all blacks, however, believe this strategy of "power confrontation" is the best way to deal with racist or abusive speech, or that they need a "fighting words" doctrine to protect them from certain forms of discriminatory harassment. Alan Keyes, a former U.S. assistant secretary of state, told a civil-rights symposium at Stanford in March 1990 that he was insulted that, as a black man, he should be made to feel he was incapable of defending himself. The basic problem with all these attempts to protect minorities, women, homosexuals, and various other groups, he said, is that "the protection incapacitates and weakens the very people the regulations intend to protect. Furthermore, their patronizing, paternalistic arguments are often base. To think," he went on, "that I will sit here in a chair and be told that white folks have the moral character to shrug off insults, and I do not, and that I will not take this as an insult? I do," Keyes said. "That is the most insidious, the most insulting, the most racist statement of all."

Keyes asserted that the most important aspects of a university education are the pursuit of truth and the preparation of students to become citizens. Protecting certain groups from harassment, he declared, violates both concerns. "Is discrimination something that is supposed to prepare you to seek truth, to pursue it and to persist in that endeavor despite obstacles? Is that something from which I should be protected, or is it something for which I wish to be prepared? If I step out of Stanford University and the first time I get into a debate with a real gutter fighter on any issue of importance, and he looks at me and calls me a nigger, and I lose my mind, you ask me whether I should not come back to Stanford and seek a refund?" Keyes asked. "This particular form of protection will leave the protected ones weaker on their own behalf," he said. "It will institutionalize their victimization because it will leave them in a position unprepared to fight for themselves against it. Education has to offer something more, and particularly to those who wish to be free. Freedom is, in essence, the ability to defend yourself."[8]

Keyes received a standing ovation from the mostly white audience. A Stanford professor who had heard his address later remarked that it was a "very moving moment. I'll tell you something else," he added. "That speech could only have been given by a black man. If a white speaker had made those comments, he wouldn't have been greeted with wild applause. He'd have gotten boos and catcalls, or maybe just dead silence. That tells me something about who can speak frankly and honestly on this campus about race or race-related matters."

The truth is that talking openly about race, either on or off a college campus, is something a great many people have neither the will nor the desire to do. Many white students at Stanford frequently said that they held back their opinions because, as one of them put it, "It's easier to keep your mouth shut than having constantly to deny you're a racist." Two white women, one of whom had lived for a year in Ujamaa and the other in Casa Zapata (the Chicano dormitory), agreed that in a multiracial setting it was difficult to discuss such issues as "diversity" or affirmative action or whether students should be required to take more ethnic-studies courses "without having the whole discussion turn into a debate about racism." As one of them observed, "Sure, it's an important problem, and it's talked about all the time here. But that doesn't mean all these other issues must always be reduced to racism or sexism, does it? After a while it gets a little tiresome. Instead of bringing us together, it just polarizes us more, and that only makes people suspicious and afraid of those who are different from them."

Nor is it easy to discuss in any public forum (and sometimes even in small informal settings) how members of diverse racial groups may be "different" from one another. "I can see as a white man that I'm different from a black man," said a Stanford sophomore, "but I'd like to know if what I can see for myself is important or not. Are we *really* different from each other—and if so, how and why? Maybe I'm wrong in the differences I see. Okay, then I need to find that out, right? What I usually hear," he went on, "is that we can't compare these differences because the standards of comparison are biased. In other words, I don't see what I think I do because it's only my subjective judgment, my own personal prejudice, which then ends up being called racism. It's weird. Why can't people be tolerant of each other and still admit we may have differences in what we think and believe? If I can't ask questions like this while I'm at Stanford— I mean, basic questions about race—where else am I going to get the answers?"

Those who have argued that campus racism is widespread have been guided by a number of assumptions they have incorporated into their habits of thought and action, either as active principles or as truths tacitly accepted as "the way things are" or as "the way things ought to be." Many of these assumptions have grown up around certain "magic words" with variable meanings—"diversity," "multiculturalism," "pluralism," "Eurocentrism," "role models," "oppression"—which, to borrow the language of historian Carl Becker, "slip off the tongue or the pen without fear and without research, words that are unconsciously mistaken for objective realities."[9] For example, it is regularly asserted that affirmative action is merely an attempt to make up for our past sins as a racist society—and then there often follows the familiar dictum that echoed black activist Stokeley Carmichael's in the 1960s: "If you are not actively with us, you are actively against us." However, as one begins to examine these assumptions, along with the many unqualified assertions that ensue, one quickly runs into a large measure of misrepresentation and distortion. Race relations in our colleges and universities are far more complex than many observers are wont to conceive them to be, especially when assumptions are made that are believed to be so unremarkable and obvious as hardly to require discussion or proof. Yet, almost inevitably, there are opposite and contradictory assumptions that lead to very different conclusions. To dismiss these assumptions out of hand is to misinterpret the cumulative pressures with which a campus must deal under circumstances of rapid change and conflict. In these cases—where sets of opposing assumptions exist—it may well be that the counterassertions turn out to be more decisive and to carry more weight when thrown into the scale.

Consider a number of assumptions and assertions about race-related issues at Stanford (and other campuses as well) as they are set down together in the following listing:

1. The educational problems of blacks and other minorities are the result of widespread discrimination. The solution is to have more-energetic and single-minded enforcement of affirmative-action programs, based on race and ethnicity, that require a form of proportional representation of certain minority groups in student admissions.

But: Many of the problems of minority groups are no longer the result of discrimination. Legal discrimination against blacks or Hispanic-Americans is not of much consequence in the area of educational opportunity. Yet if the deeper social and economic problems that confront minorities today are treated as if they are simply problems of discrimination, the outcome will be growth of the quota mentality everywhere.

2. Statistics do not lie. Blacks, Hispanic-Americans and other minority groups are not heavily represented on university faculties. The situation will not improve unless our colleges and universities move to bring about a statistically acceptable representation of minorities on their faculties.

But: The low incidence of minority faculty representation is not the result of invariable discrimination. These same statistics, by themselves, do not explain *why* there is low minority representation. The principal reason is limited supply. The idea that one can legitimately infer discrimination from a discrepancy in the ratio of minority members employed to the total population is simply inappropriate for institutions of higher education. What needs to be done to deal with this situation is to get black and Hispanic youngsters to take math and science courses rather than social or ethnic studies. One reason Asian-Americans have forged ahead in recent decades in getting good jobs and higher income is that they have concentrated in the sciences, mathematics, engineeering, and architecture even though they have faced severe discrimination.

3. "Excellence" should not be the primary concern of the university because it works to exclude minorities. Instead, the university should be concerned with "adequacy," defined by Harvard professor of education Charles Willie as "that which is sufficient to meet the requirements of the situation." The university should aim to certify that all those passing through its gates are "good enough to help but not bad enough to harm." Any talk of a master university smacks of a master race. Many whites who are highly qualified will have to make room for those qualified on the basis of other kinds of "intelligence."[10]

But: Recommendations to "rescue" members of minority groups from the requirements and goals of academic excellence are a recipe for mediocrity as well as for double standards. Such proposals—no matter how often they are bathed in the warm light of "diversity" and "pluralism"—are demeaning to minority students who do not wish to be treated as exceptions to legitimate academic requirements.

4. Long-established hiring standards and "frozen formulas" of traditional scholarship are applied so stringently as to exclude minority applicants and keep the number of minority faculty appointments disproportionately low. To diversify their faculties, colleges and universities must reconsider the importance of the Ph.D. in recruiting minority candidates, especially since there are many more black and minority students who hold master's degrees than Ph.D.s. In addition to asking why a Ph.D. is required to teach, it is necessary to incorporate into the faculty hiring process equivalency criteria such as community service or working in a social agency as ways of attracting more minorities. Plans should also be developed that would not only suspend temporarily the hiring of qualified white males but hold faculty positions open until members of certain minority groups can be found to fill them. The objective of affirmative action is equalized results.[11]

But: Affirmative action is not simply a program that yields

gains and benefits. It also entails demonstrable costs and consequences. To believe otherwise is to fail to understand that what one person gains under affirmative action may well be taken away from someone else. The notion of equal results is especially objectionable when it is seen to be abandoning the principle of individual merit and accomplishment that is central to the integrity of higher education.

The suggestion that there are teachers available who do not have Ph.D.'s is irrelevant. The traditional criterion for hiring faculty at first-class institutions is the Ph.D. Even if adequate criteria to measure teacher performance existed, we could still fill the classrooms with Ph.D.'s. Furthermore, to establish different qualifications so that we have first- and second-class faculty appointments, with minority-group members constituting second-class faculty—that in itself would be a disaster.

Virtually everyone in higher education agrees that minorities should finally have equal access to all the jobs that for so long had been denied them. But to adopt a policy that grants preferential "set-asides" in faculty hiring to certain groups solely on the basis of race is to put into practice a discriminatory system of quotas.

5. One of the truths of our times is that because we are all products of our culture, we are to a large degree also products of our race, especially insofar as our race has a strong and distinct cultural implication. To ignore race is to strip African-Americans of a powerful component of their personality. Indeed, "ignoring" race assigns maximum importance to the dominant culture by implicitly asking minorities to adopt the majority culture and therefore lose their own identity. The notion that "We are all the same under the skin" really means in practice "We are all white under the skin." Since there is little of "self" beyond culture, personal identity is a group-based concept that is tied closely to minority- or majority-ness.

But: The philosophy that gave the civil-rights movement its moral authority and political appeal is that race does not—or should not—matter. Race is an accidental characteristic, irrelevant to our common human purposes. As Isaac Barchas, a senior in classics, wrote in the *Stanford Daily* in 1989, "What divides the races is trivial compared to what unites the species. What matters is not that one is black or white, but that one is a human being." The unit of analysis is not the group but the individual, "and people who hold this philosophy emphasize human unity and reject a person's minority or majority status as incidental to individual expression."

6. To raise the self-esteem of black students, a more "Afrocentric" curriculum that emphasizes black culture and black history must be developed in our colleges and universities. Students must become familiar with the history of their race or nationality if they are to develop pride in themselves. As the New York State Board of Education's Task Force on Minorities has stated, children from minority cultures will have higher self-esteem and self-respect if all curricular materials including math and science are prepared on the basis of this focus and emphasis. It is the best way to give the individual student a chance to construct a genuine identity.

But: Self-esteem is not the most important educational gift we can give to young students. When, recently, the California Task Force to Promote Self-Esteem said that "life's about everyone getting A's, not about some normal distribution curve," it was not talking about life on *this* planet. If life teaches us anything, it is that everyone does *not* get A's. It is important for black students to know about the history of black peoples and Africa, and for Hispanic children to know something about their own culture. But too much emphasis has been placed on making students feel good about themselves. Real and lasting self-esteem does not come from teaching children in school to feel good about what little math they know, but from teaching them how to multiply and divide. The success of Chinese students in math is due not to a "Sinocentric" approach to numbers but to hard work. For most children, self-esteem—specifically, the self-confidence that grows out of having reached a goal—comes not from hearing about what their ancestors did, but from what *they* have been able to accomplish through their own efforts.[12]

Furthermore, the sense of cultural community that the "Afro-centric" movement is attempting to create is based on a myth of uniqueness, along with strenuous efforts to develop "black pride." While the movement may have led to some success in the political arena, such as mobilizing students to pursue their goals defined by a leadership that preaches the doctrine of perpetual victimhood, it has not produced the same educational success when measured by individual performance in the classroom. According to UC-Berkeley anthropologist John Ogbu, a black "oppositional" subculture has developed around a set of assumptions and attitudes from which individual and group identity are defined in overt opposition to white culture, resulting in an adverse educational effect on many blacks, since to succeed is often considered "acting white."

7. Racism is the single undeniable fact of life in every corner of the United States. In the words of Syd Finley, executive director of the Chicago chapter of the NAACP, it is "as American as apple pie and mother. It determines who has an equal chance to succeed and who will be excluded from the mainstream economic and social networks. Everything affecting our relationships is defined by race. For over two hundred years, whites have clung to negative racial stereotypes about blacks, which have confirmed their beliefs that blacks are inferior. In order to confront the continuing plight of the black underclass, the central problem of African-Americans, we must first recognize that racism, according to the Rev. Ralph D. Abernathy, is stronger

today than it was in the 1950s and '60s.

But: The black underclass in America would not disappear if racism were eradicated tomorrow. Although racism is real enough, it has also been a "destructive myth" for blacks by giving greater power to the odds against success than exist in reality, as *Washington Post* columnist William Raspberry has stated. "It encourages the fallacy," he says, "that to attack racism as the source of our problems is the same as attacking our problems. As a result, we expend precious resources—time, energy, imagination, political capital—searching (always successfully) for evidence of racism, while our problems grow worse."[13]

8. Racist acts on college campuses have been increasing in number in recent years, with new incidents and controversies arising almost daily. Things will not change (according to a memorandum circulated at Tulane University) unless "several basic assumptions" are accepted, the most important of which is that "racism is pervasive" and "fundamentally present" and will be difficult to root out "because we are all the progeny of a racist society." Like a weed, racism keeps growing back, says Prof. Clayborne Carson of Stanford University, an authority on African-American history and editor of the Martin Luther King Jr. papers. In the 1960s, when there was an active effort to stamp it out, "the civil-rights movement made students involved and interested. The education process was ongoing. In the last ten years, that education process has ground to a halt."

But: The larger truth is that virtually every respectable college and university has gone out of its way in the last ten years to recruit an increasing number of black and other minority students and to try to develop a campus environment of support for them. Instead of grinding to a halt, the "education process" has moved quickly and determinedly to develop what one Stanford administrator candidly describes as a "new political-action program" that at institutions across the country has produced (among other initiatives): a growth of race-based affirmative-action programs that blacks themselves have insisted on, vigorous efforts in behalf of "multiculturalism" (including a growing number of courses in "minority cultures" added to the curriculum), and "racial-awareness seminars" and forums designed to deal with allegations of student and faculty "discriminatory attitudes" and "insensitivity" toward blacks and other minorities. There are few institutions of higher education that have not publicly comitted themselves to campus-wide initiatives that seek "race enrichment" as part of a greater effort to "change the character of the university and to bring it to the next level of social and human progress."

Moreover, it is sometimes difficult to escape the conclusion that the public handling of race-related issues has increasingly come to signify the limited extent to which university administrations share the putatively progressive values of tolerance, an absence of ethnocentrism, and a belief in nondiscrimination. A refusal to yield to pressures on faculty hiring—for example, by declaring that the appointment of the best-qualified persons without regard to race or gender is correct in principle—is likely to result in a college president being labeled an "obstructionist" unwilling to break down the barriers to "participation of peoples of color in formerly all-white-male bastions." To suggest that some students are too sensitive to what they take to be harmful speech is to communicate racial insensitivity. Since administrators are anxious to convey the message "We're with you and we share the concerns that inspire your protests, even if not always agreeing in every detail with your tactical positions," they end up acquiescing in actions which they should, in fact, be opposing on principled grounds. It is no small irony that in their desire to send the "right" signal to their liberal activist constituencies, these administrators are impelled to act in ways that are contrary to some of the most fundamental and classical liberal values. To affirm the principle that blacks should not be segregated, and that in the interest of creating a genuinely liberal environment black students should (even over their own objections) be assigned to campus housing without regard to race or color, would be virtually impossible for any college administrator who wants to avoid being thought of as some kind of political reactionary.

Is there a "new racism" at Stanford? And if so, is it new in the sense that its character is different from the form it took fifty or even thirty years ago? Or is it even a resurgence of the old-fashioned racism in its familiar social pattern? The evidence does not point to an onrush of racist offenses. In the personal interviews, the actual number of black students who could give specific examples of racist behavior they had experienced or observed was very low. A number of blacks reported that they had encountered students who displayed various manifestations of what they perceived as racially motivated antagonisms, but the racism involved was generally "subtle," hard to define, and even harder to express in words. Although they came face-to-face with very few racists, a great many blacks said they felt they "didn't fit in" at Stanford and were not understood. For these black students—but not for all black students—their sense of estrangement is a problem. But is it racism?[14]

In considering the possible causes of these negative feelings, it is important to recall that as many as eight out of ten black students say they have experienced racism before attending Stanford. In addition, they are acutely aware of the virulent racism their parents and grandparents were forced to endure. To these sons and daughters, therefore, the presence of racism is for all practical purposes a given, and the battle for civil rights waged by past generations a legacy of pride. Thus their own history and knowledge have caused today's black students— the first black students to grow up in an America that grants all blacks full legal rights—to make the continuing struggle against the racism they anticipate and abhor central to black consciousness. To give full expression to their black identity, they must demonstrate their unwavering opposition to white racism, which is why, at Stanford or at any other university, the black experience and the commitment to a full agenda of anti-racist activities are inextricably linked.

Not surprisingly, most white students at Stanford have had a far different experience. Only a small number of them have lived or socialized with blacks or other minorities before arriving on campus. They have read and heard about the civil-rights movement—"about the way it used to be," as one of them stated—but for the most part they do not have memories of the turbulent Sixties. "I wasn't even born when Martin Luther King was shot," a white junior observed. While they acknowledge the seriousness of the problem on campus, they do not see themselves or the University as racist. "The great tragedy is that four years at Stanford isn't solving the problem," remarked a graduating senior. "Whites and blacks do not understand one another. As freshmen, we are all taught the value of diversity and a multicultural student body. Time passes, and the core track in liberal arts is changed to incorporate more 'ethnic' thought. In the process we learn that blacks feel oppressed. We also learn," he added, "that the black community on campus values separateness. But that seems so incongruous. How can it be that black students come to a university that is striving for integration and equality, yet they refuse to socialize with whites?"

The answer, of course, is that many blacks on campus are not really seeking integration. They are looking for power, what one of them described as the "new power that is the responsibility of our generation." Whites do not realize that in their self-segregation, blacks are expressing both their individuality and their unity in what they feel is the strength that comes from difference and independence. When an ugly incident occurs—when, for example, blacks find an offensive poster hung in the

Afro-American theme house—tensions quickly rise. The black students are hurt and angry. The white students are not quite sure what to do. With the black rage come more demands for changes in the structure and "power centers" of the university, along with demands for more education suited to their needs, more courses in ethnic studies and non-Western cultures. And, also, blacks withdraw even further into their own community. Whites are confused, fearful of identifying themselves with any racist element, and eventually angered again by the blacks' move to self-separation. The white students grow less sympathetic to the "anti-racist" courses added to the curriculum, and blacks easily interpret the lack of support as overt opposition or callous apathy.

So, after all, is there a new racism? There can be no doubt that circumstances are new in the sense that conditions and events are historically unequaled. This is the first generation of students since the watershed years of the Civil Rights Act and the Voting Rights Act of the 1960s, the first generation since the country rededicated itself to its long-standing ideals of equality and justice for all Americans. As for racial matters, the nation and its people have changed radically in the span of three decades. A group of talented children was born in the Sixties. Some were black, some were white. While growing up, they learned different lessons unique to their own times and experiences. As mature young adults, many of them met for the first time on a university campus, and strange and unfamiliar things started to happen.

"New," yes. But racism? At Stanford and campuses across the country, relations between black and white students are a cause of constant concern. And who could deny that there are outbursts of racism from bigots who engage in personal attacks on blacks and other minorities, or that racial tension is frequently a problem, or that there are "racist incidents," or that white and black students still have much to learn from each other? The dean of students at Columbia University, Roger Lehecka, asks, "Is there a problem in this country with the ease in which white people can make blacks invisible? Yes. But," he continues, "does that mean Columbia is a racist institution? No." As Lynn Bailiff, a psychologist in UC-Berkeley's Office of Undergraduate Affairs, has stated, what has emerged in recent years is not an increase in racism, but a growing unwillingness to tolerate it. "Berkeley hasn't put up with bigotry or harassment for quite a long time."

More often than not, suggestions of racism that are so frequently reported in the press offer excitement at the expense of the truth. "What does it mean to say we're 'racist'?" asks UC-Berkeley history professor Sheldon Rothblatt. "It's the rhetoric of the street. It's inaccurate. But I guess you don't get headlines with a little bit of this and a little bit of that." There is not much drama or excitement in describing the tensions between black and white students at Stanford and other campuses as largely a function of their inability to understand one another—more precisely, the failure of whites to understand the nature of black consciousness, and the pronounced tendency of blacks to self-segregate rather than to communicate. But it is a far more accurate description than one that would have us believe that American colleges and universities—and white students in particular—are inherently racist.

There are, of course, many students and faculty members who tie the charge of "racism" to an outlook or ideology that views the fundamental workings of the world (and the university) in racial terms, in much the same way that for Marxists the world is based on class and the class struggle. They maintain that American society—and whites in particular—is steeped in racism. "That's a lot to load on an 18-year-old," says political scientist Jean Elshtain of the University of Massachusetts at Amherst. As a number of the interviews with Stanford students revealed, many white students resent being told all year long that they are racists. A sophomore at the Massachusetts Institute of Technology from Brooklyn, New York, expressed the same sentiment: "I grew up with white, yellow, black. I mean half my buddies on the football team were black, and I come here and read every other day in the paper I'm a racist. It irritates me."[15]

It cannot be said too often that the whole issue of race on campus, as the *Christian Science Monitor's* Robert Marquand reported, "is far more complicated and elusive than simply a resurgence of white-on-black bias—the popular view, born of journalism" that, as Harvard sociologist David Riesman puts it, "simplistically filters the story through a 1960s civil-rights framework." The word "racism" itself, he points out, is charged with emotional associations and is often used irresponsibly. It becomes, along with "bigotry," a tool for playing racial politics. Its original meaning assumed racial superiority, "but that is very different from ignorance, insensitivity, or even prejudice." Many of the familiar charges of racism were based on single-incident stories—physical assaults, contemptuous name-calling, racial graffiti—and many of these episodes (several of which were later found to be dubious or untrue) were connected to alcohol, campus parties, or sporting events. Some stories that received national attention were sparked by a handful of students on campuses of more than 20,000. What is left out of these "incident stories" is a whole set of new circumstances on today's campuses that are significantly different from campus conditions in the late 1970s or early 1980s. There are new problems and, along with them, new tensions and pressures. There is no more important problem (or one more indicative of the "new times") than what Marquand has described as "the cultural dynamic among blacks themselves—their effort to establish an identity on campus (should they be more 'black' or more mainstream?), and a new black political assertiveness brought forth partly by student activists and partly by radical or ideological black faculty."[16]

Few students or campus officials would deny that race is a problem, if only because they have seen it emerge in so many different forms. In a letter to the student *Daily* in early 1989, a Stanford alumnus (class of 1987) aired a sentiment often voiced in the one-on-one personal interviews when he took strong exception to the argument that a person's skin color devalues his opinion regarding minority issues. He referred specifically to the notion he had seen recently expressed in the *Daily* that white people could never understand the problems of blacks "because they are white, and whites should admit that." He readily conceded that whites cannot empathize completely with the experience of blacks and other minorities who have suffered racial discrimination but, he said, "as human beings we share many characteristics, among them the ability to sympathize with and understand people who have undergone experiences quite unlike our own. Just because one cannot empathize completely with someone else's experience does not mean that one cannot understand it at all. Indeed, if the latter were the case," he went on, "there would seem little reason for communication between human beings at all, since each of us experiences a life different from anyone else's."

The feeling is shared by most white students at Stanford, for whom the goal is mutual understanding through closer personal relations and who, it can be justly said, are not guilty of racist or discriminatory practices. The great majority, in fact, are trying to combat the vestiges of such behavior. They are frustrated, however, when the struggle is so frequently defined as the struggle of "people of color against whites." To those black students who claim that whites belong to the "oppressor group" and are unable "to connect" with their history or culture, their answer is that blacks do not give whites enough credit. Important changes have taken place in the last several decades, and, in particular, white attitudes have shifted from widespread acceptance of segregation and discrimination as recently as the 1940s and 1950s to a new and equally widespread commitment to tolerance and racial equality. While many of the black leaders stress the power that can come only from their unity and solidarity as a cohesive campus group, many of the most-thoughtful white students believe that no positive end will be achieved unless all individuals judge each other individually. If there are white students on campus who act in a prejudiced or racist manner, there are many more who behave decently and fairly.

One of the great ironies to emerge from the civil-rights movement is that while whites today are asked to raise their own consciousness so that they will no longer think or act as members of a racial group (as, for example, when "white supremacy" was riding high), many blacks are increasingly defining themselves more distinctly in group terms and have made race consciousness the center of their identity. "How else are we going to use our power to change things around here when the system of white control is already stacked against us?" asked a black junior at Stanford. White students, however, believe that the argument is a misreading of the situation on campus. They do not see themselves—nor do they see the university as an institution—as a powerful force bent on advancing "white" interests. Moreover, the principles many of them have sought to embrace are reflected in a vision of America—"It's what I learned from reading Martin Luther King," a white history major at Stanford declared—in which race would disappear as a reasonable or reliable consideration in the treatment of individuals. Stanford's University Committee on Minority Issues spoke in a similar fashion when it began its report by affirming its belief in "a humanistic value of respect for our fellow human beings. Ethnic differences . . . should present us singular opportunities to find mutual understanding and respect." If one talks with so-called "average" students—and not simply with student activists, who always assert a proprietary claim over campus political issues, including race relations—it becomes clear that most of them believe that the best hope for harmonious interaction rests on the willingness of individuals to refuse to draw exclusive boundaries around their "partial identities" as blacks or whites. A graduating white senior, speaking in more personal terms, said that "the fight I would like to see waged against bigotry and prejudice on campus is through friendship. That's the only way we can break down the barriers and really come together."[17]

In the hour-long conversations with students (and white students in particular, although not exclusively), the observation was repeatedly made in one form or another that the concept of race is and should be irrelevant in making a friend or judging a human being. Many of them said they had been taught by their high-school teachers that to eliminate any discriminatory barriers or practices, it is necessary to create a climate in which color and background are invalid issues. They also learned how vitally important it is to appreciate the multicultural nature of American society. Since becoming Stanford undergraduates, however, they have discovered that race has become an increasingly dominant factor in shaping the campus environment. "I played on our football team in high school, and that's where I really learned about color-blindness," a white sophomore commented. "But that's not talked about much here. The only goal you hear about now is diversity. Everything's tied to diversity. No one seems to care, though, that diversity isn't always color-blind. It can also be very race-conscious. It can even be discriminatory."

A wise observer of the human scene, Professor Paul A. Freund of the Harvard Law School (now retired), likes to quote Lord Acton's statement that "an absolute principle is as absurd as absolute power." Professor Freund's own rule is equally simple and clear: "When you perceive a truth, look for the balancing truth." It is true that black and white students at Stanford frequently complain about the racial situation, and that black-white relations are often strained and tense. But it is also true that the sentiment among most white students reveals a reservoir of good will, and that a great many of them undertake special efforts to promote racial harmony and social integration. It is true that things sometimes get out of hand and that charges are frequently made that all minority problems on campus are the fault of the "racist system." But it is even more true, as John Warfield, a black professor of education and of Afro-American studies at the University of Texas has stated, that "the academic community is not especially racist. I don't think black kids in college today are having an organically racist experience. A silly white boy on the radio making a racial slur is not quite the same thing as having to march to open up the institution, or get at gate-keeping ideologies. It pales with previous experiences."[18]

If there is one predominant finding regarding racial attitudes on campus, it is that the great majority of white students have shown in many different ways that they pay little attention to, and will not follow the lead of, those who carry a message of racial hostility toward blacks or other minorities. However, it has not always been easy for many whites to adjust to the "new diversity" of today's student body or, in particular, the growth of black consciousness. Indeed, for some of them it has been a bewildering and, on occasion, painful experience. But the fundamental change and fact of life on campus—irrespective of the bigotry and prejudice that may still exist—is the normative definition and expectation of how blacks and whites should relate to each other. Stated simply, most white students today believe that blacks deserve the same treatment and respect as whites. One may argue about whether these sentiments represent real "inner change" by white students, or if they merely provide a deceptively attractive appearance that obscures a continuing and deep-seated racism. This is not an easy question to answer— but it is also not necessarily the only or critical question. It is worth keeping in mind that "all of us conform to norms that we may or may not have internalized, but which guide our actions in ways that are of considerable consequence for our relations with others."[19]

While race relations at Stanford and on other campuses are often marked by tension and are sometimes stretched to the limit, the most-thoughtful white students agree with Martin Luther King Jr.'s conviction that the surest way to achieve rights for black Americans is to understand how those rights were so long denied "and to change them through friendship."

Footnotes

Chapter 1 Footnotes

[1] Shelby Steele, "The Recoloring of Campus Life," *Harper's Magazine*, February 1989, pp. 47–55.

Chapter 2 Footnotes

[1] After a three-year period in which Asian-American applicants to Stanford were admitted at a rate only 65 to 70 percent of the Caucasian admission rate, Stanford's 1986 Asian-American rate rose to 89 percent of its Caucasian admission rate. Combined with a higher proportion of Asian-American admittees choosing to enroll at Stanford (50 percent in 1985, 63 percent in 1986), this resulted in a more than 100 percent increase in Asian-Americans enrolled in Stanford's 1986 freshman class (119 in 1985 and 245 in 1986).

[2] Applications to Stanford in 1990 came from 4,128 different high schools (down from 4,668 high schools in 1989). The admitted class came from 1,540 different high schools (up from 1,534 a year ago). The total number of applications, 12,950, was a 13.2 percent decrease from 1989, reflecting the continued national decline of high-school graduates that is projected to continue through the mid-1990s.

[3] Included among the demands was that an Ethnic Studies graduation requirement be instituted, the immediate hiring of a black history professor and a black political-science professor, a commitment to setting aside at least half of the newly created Centennial faculty positions for "faculty of color," the strengthening of the fundamental standard to include a clause that clearly states that "racist acts are a violation of the fundamental standard," "an end to the practice of 'last hired, first fired' for black workers," and eight student trustees—four at large and one each from the black, Chicano, Asian, and American Indian communities.

Chapter 4 Footnotes

[1] These reports are related to the students' self-identified political views. Thus 75 percent of "very liberal" seniors say they have seen racism on campus, compared to 14 percent of "very conservative" seniors. Seventy-seven percent of "very liberal" minority respondents say they have been the target of racism, whereas only 39 percent of "somewhat conservative" minority students make the same claim. Much larger percentages—over 80 percent of both minority and non-minority students—say they had either seen racism or been the target of racism *before* enrolling at Stanford.

[2] According to those who use the library on a regular basis, this is not a particularly good example of racism on the campus. It is common practice for students to be stopped at the inspection booth every time they leave the library. It is very unlikely that Ivy was the victim of a racist act.

Chapter 7 Footnotes

[1] A fuller exposition of the "symbolic racism" thesis can be found in John B. McConahay and Joseph C. Hough, "Symbolic Racism," *Journal of Social Issues* 3 (2) (1976), pp. 23–45, and Donald R. Kinder and Davis O. Sears, "Prejudice and Politics: Symbolic Racism Versus Racial Threats to the Good Life," *Journal of Personality and Social Psychology* 40 (1981), pp. 414–31. For a

critical assessment of "symbolic racism," see two articles by Byron M. Roth: "Symbolic Racism: The Making of a Scholarly Myth," *Academic Questions,* Summer 1989, and "Social Psychology's Racism," *The Public Interest,* Winter 1990.

[2] For a more complete analysis of the "new racism," see the perceptive analysis by Thomas Short that appeared in the August 1988 issue of *Commentary* magazine.

[3] For a discussion (without the usual political polemics) of the changes that were made in the freshman course involving the eight different "tracks," as well as a more general analysis of the arguments from those who oppose the traditional conceptions of liberal education, see UC-Berkeley professor of philosophy John Searle's excellent article "The Storm Over the University" in *The New York Review,* December 6, 1990.

[4] It is by way of affirming the importance of Western ideas and values to America that Saul Bellow's comment that "when the Zulus have a Tolstoy, we will read him" should be understood.

[5] Two extensive summaries of the report can be found in Carl Irving's account in the *San Francisco Examiner,* September 9, 1990 ("Study Outlines Racial Barriers at UC Berkeley"), and in *The New York Times,* November 20, 1990 ("Berkeley: Diverse But Still Divided").

[6] There is an even more important consideration in any discussion of white ethnic Americans that, regrettably, the faculty study did not take into account. As Alan Wolfe, professor of sociology and political science and dean of the Graduate Faculty at the New School for Social Research, points out, ethnicity barely exists among white ethnics. "The great majority of ethnic Americans are intermarried, participate rarely in the culture of their inherited ethnicity, do not pass on their ethnic heritage to their children, and consider themselves, in actual behavior if not always in nostalgic reminiscence, fully American." While racial minorities are insisting on their racial differences, "white ethnics are discovering that their historical identities are less distinctive." See Professor Wolfe's book review-essay, "The Return of the Melting Pot" in the *New Republic,* December 31, 1990.

[7] The statements quoted here are from an article entitled "Fighting Words" by San Francisco Bay Area writer Ira Eisenberg, which appeared in the "This World" section of the *San Francisco Chronicle* of September 9, 1990.

[8] This account of Mr. Keyes' comments appeared in Stanford University's weekly publication *Campus Report*, March 21, 1990.

[9] Carl Becker, *The Heavenly City of the Eighteenth Century Philosophers* (New Haven: Yale University Press, 1932), p. 47. For a discussion of the way the "soft amalgam of assumptions"operates to fix the pattern of American culture, see Robert S. Lynd, *Knowledge for What?* (Princeton: Princeton University Press, 1946), pp. 54–113.

[10] Furthermore, a university such as UC-Berkeley is justified in turning away white and Asian students with straight-A averages in the spirit of affirmative action ("institutionalized compassion") and in the name of "diversity." All of these assertions were made by Charles Willie at a conference entitled "From the Eurocentric University to the Multicultural University: The Faculty's Challenge for the Twenty-First Century" held in Oakland, California, in October 1989. Professor Willie's address was called "Equity and Excellence."

[11] These proposals were made to the Chancellor's Council of Presidents of the California State University system by three staff members of the U.S. Commission on Civil Rights on May 25, 1972. For a more complete discussion of their recommendations for higher education, see my "Minority Faculty Hiring: Problems and Prospects" in *The American Scholar*, Winter, 1990, pp. 39–52.

[12] For a more extended version of this analysis of race and ethnicity in American education—and one of the best in the literature—see Diane Ravitch, "Multiculturalism: E Pluribus Plures," *The American Scholar*, Summer 1990, pp. 337–354.

[13] Of the columnist William Raspberry, *TIME* magazine once wrote that he is "the most respected black voice on any white U.S. newspaper. Not surprisingly, his judgment regularly nettles the Pollyannas and the militants." His comments are from "A Journalist's view of Black Economics" in *The Free Market And The Black Community* (Hillsdale: Hillsdale College Press, 1990), pp. 66–69.

[14] Before Chancellor Ira Heyman retired in 1990, he asked UC-Berkeley professor Troy Duster to find out what students were actually experiencing in terms of racial hostilities on the Berkeley campus. As reported by Ira Eisenberg in the *San Francisco Chronicle*, September 9, 1990, Duster spent a year interviewing a wide cross-section of students and came up with some remarkably revealing insights: "What I experienced when I talked to these kids is their increasing

rage at their own inability to justify the charges of racism. *We* knew what racism was," he observed, referring to the events of his own generation, which grew up before the Civil Rights Act of 1964. But among black and other minority students today, "there's no longer any agreement on what constitutes racism." Duster frequently heard complaints of racism, but when he probed for details, he said, "what I'd get is a kind of choking up. A stutter would start, then impoverished, inarticulate vocabulary. They couldn't quite put their finger on what it is that would let me or anybody else know that that's what it is—that's racism." Eisenberg, *op. cit.* Even the new "subtle racism" that whites are accused of is hard to define. "I feel racism all around me," said a professor of Afro-American studies at the University of Massachusetts, "but it's hard to pin down. It's like AIDS. Ask most people if there's an AIDS problem, and they'll say they don't feel it. But people who have AIDS say otherwise."

[15] Quotations are from Robert Marquand, *op. cit.*

[16] One of the most balanced and discerning treatments of campus racism can be found in the two-part series by Robert Marquand in the *Christian Science Monitor* of June 14 and 15, 1988. Still another insightful analysis is by Charles A. Radin of the *Boston Globe*, 1988. Several of the professors' comments cited here are from these accounts.

[17] There are some barriers, it seems that even friendship cannot cross. A black Stanford student, Marcus Mabry, told a moving story of how he was teaching blacks and whites (while a resident assistant in a freshman dormitory) the importance of "being treated the same while I was approaching them differently." "Once,"he wrote in *Newsweek* magazine, "a close white friend said the word 'nigger' when he, one of his best friends (also black), and I were in my room. The other black guy and I said that it was OK for him to say 'nigger' with just the three of us around, but he could never say it with others in earshot." Mabry explained that no white could "ever enter that fraternity because no white could ever know the pain of being black." His white friend, he said, "felt the walls of prejudice closing in and suffocating him, dividing him from us. Tears welled up in my friend's eyes as he said, 'I try so hard, I love you guys.'" Mabry said he never got over "what we had done to him that night. We had separated him from us the way we had been separated so often." For the first time in his life his white friend "felt the vulnerability that only having the wrong skin color at the wrong time can bring." It is highly ironic, Mabry reflected, that "only whites who care enough to have black relationships open themselves to getting hurt so much."

[18] Quotation in Marquand, *op. cit.*

[19] This point is made in *Racial Attitudes in America* by Howard Schuman, Charlotte Steeh, and Lawrence Bobo (Harvard University Press, 1985), p. 203.

Appendix:

Ethnic Theme Houses at Stanford

U nlike many of the changes at Stanford whose
origins lay in the political activism and
heightened consciousness that followed soon
after the death of Martin Luther King Jr. in
1968—such as the effort to admit more
minority students and hire more minority faculty,
the development of special remedial programs
for minority admittees, and the creation of a
program in African and Afro-American Studies—
the establishment of ethnic theme houses occurred
with relatively little debate.

(This article first appeared in the Summer and Fall 1985 issues of *Stanford Magazine*. I wish
to acknowledge the invaluable research assistance of Jeanne J. Fleming, who received her
Ph.D. in sociology from Stanford in 1982.)

Since the first black students were admitted (one or two as early as the 1920s), Stanford's policy had been to scatter them as widely as possible among the various campus residences so as to afford the maximum number of white students an opportunity to get to know black students and black culture, and to encourage black students to make white friends and learn about white culture in a university setting. That, it was felt, was what an integrated education was all about.

During the early 1970s the ideal of integration came under attack. There were fewer than 250 black students at Stanford in 1972 (out of close to 6,500 undergraduates), and many of them complained about the effect of being spread very thinly throughout the dormitories. In the words of one black administrator, "They felt uncomfortably like guinea pigs in the University's efforts to educate whites about blacks, and were tired of going home at night to be observed and questioned."

Official race barriers had begun to fall at colleges and universities during the 1960s. Only a few years later, however, black pride, black power, and black nationalism were in the air. On many campuses black students demonstrated (sometimes violently) as they sought to affirm their own identity and self-esteem and to help define the concept of "black consciousness." For many it was a period of "cultural shock"—the powerful sense of isolation and inadequacy that many black college students said they felt when they came to a predominantly white campus.

Blacks began to encourage their peers to stop assimilating and imitating white standards and instead to begin to build cultural centers, where they could be free to be black. As one member of the early group of black students remembers it, what they were looking for—and what they eventually succeeded in creating—was "a sort of black neighborhood at Stanford."

In 1970–71, a group of black undergraduates approached the Office of Residential Education with a proposal to house, on an experimental basis, a substantial number of black students in one "concentration" dorm. The proposal was accepted.

The first ethnic concentration dorm began operation in the fall of 1971. About thirty black freshmen were housed in Cedro, and about the same number across the court in Junipero. Other minority groups on campus soon asked for their own dorms and, by the mid-1970s, Casa Zapata (Chicano) and Okada (Asian-American) had been established. Although the University's response to the black students' request for a concentration dorm was favorable and rapid, it drew the line at an all-black (or all-ethnic) dormitory. From the very first the University insisted that no more than 50 percent of the room space in a given dorm could be designated as an ethnic priority, a policy from which it has never significantly deviated.

The black students who approached the Office of Residential Education in 1970 were apparently not eager to develop a theme house like the academic theme houses that had been in operation on campus since the mid-1960s and whose function was to provide both those who lived there and the broader student community with exposure to different cultures. According to two of those who were active in setting up the concentration dorm, the black students were not interested in helping to further educate the white community at Stanford, nor were they at that time particularly anxious to develop a program for blacks on black history and black culture.

What they did care about was creating a "comfortable home" for people who shared a common culture, a home distinguished by its separation from white Stanford. Thus the goals of minority students and of Stanford's academic theme houses were quite dissimilar from the start. In fact, the term "theme house" was not applied to the black concentration dorm until at least a year after it was established.

Since there was no serious opposition to the black concentration dorm, it more or less slipped into the Stanford housing pattern. Although there is no official explanation of how or why the black concentration dorm evolved into a system of ethnic theme houses, one can speculate on several of the more important reasons: 1) an effort by the University to legitimate the existence of the concentration dorm; 2) the changing interests and needs of minority students who, once they had a common residence, began to think of other ways to use it—for example, by offering an alternative curriculum; 3) the changing climate of student life, with a shift from political activism to professional attainment, and from black identity to black success.

Ujamaa was the first of the ethnic theme houses and the largest (it has space for 115 students). According to Ron Hudson, assistant dean of students and current resident fellow at Ujamaa, its primary goal and major accomplishment have been to provide a place on campus for black culture to flourish. Ujamaa serves not only the needs of Stanford's black community, but as an important resource for the wider black community of Palo Alto. Among other activities, there have been a course (and some noncredit mini-seminars) on African history, programs on issues of special interest to the black community, and receptions for visiting black leaders and luminaries.

The racial breakdown at Ujamaa is approximately half black and half white. The black residents tend to be younger than the average undergraduate, largely because of the number of slots in Ujamaa specifically set aside for freshmen (40) and because black upperclassmen are inclined to seek more-independent living arrangements. Black students who live at Ujamaa are generally either those who are in transition from a black high school to white Stanford, or those who come from predominantly white neighborhoods, are middle-class, and are searching for a strong cultural identity. In the annual spring draw for the following year's campus housing, most white students historically have not expressed a preference for Ujamaa. But those who have been assigned there have found the house physically comfortable and attractive and rarely have left before the end of the academic year.

Casa Zapata, the Chicano theme house, has space for ninety students. While all of the ethnic theme houses share a common goal of providing an environment for their respective ethnic cultures to prosper and a comfortable place for their residents—especially their minority residents—to live, they are also different from each other. For example, according to James Lyons, dean of student affairs, Casa Zapata has most fully merged the functions of a cultural center and a residence and has put considerable effort into transmitting specific aspects of Hispanic culture to the entire Stanford community.

Okada, the Asian-American ethnic theme house (with room for ninety students), was the last to be established. At the time of Okada's founding in the early 1970s, the Asian-American Student Association (AASA) at Stanford was quite militant politically and Okada substantially reflected its views. But in recent years, Resident Fellow Cal Lai points out, Okada has shifted to more cultural and educational concerns and the overlap between AASA members and Okada residents has all but vanished.

Lai does not look upon Okada as a true ethnic theme house. For one thing, race is not a big issue in the house, and the racial tension that a number of observers sense in Ujamaa and Casa Zapata is not present. Furthermore, Ujamaa and Casa Zapata have stronger ties to their respective ethnic communities. Many of the supporters of Ujamaa and Casa Zapata claim that Okada has been co-opted by the white majority on campus and has therefore failed to maintain a sense of cultural identity. Okada, however, did not emerge out of the racial unrest and stridency of the late 1960s and early 1970s. It began with an intellectually oriented analysis of Japanese-American history and culture and has always benefited from considerable faculty participation.

In many important respects the three houses mirror the different positions of blacks, Hispanics, and Asian-Americans on the

Stanford campus specifically and in the rest of the country generally. In comparison to blacks and Hispanics, Asian-Americans are relatively well integrated into American society. They receive no preferential consideration or treatment in the admissions process, and they graduate with fully as many awards and honors. Put another way, of the three ethnic groups, Asian-Americans are the only ones not defined by Stanford as an affirmative-action target group.

Roble, a dormitory of some 295 students, is the Native American "priority dorm." Out of perhaps thirty undergraduate Native Americans on campus, about eight live there. The emphasis at Roble is not on an ethnic theme in daily living, but on occasionally exposing the majority residents of the dorm to different aspects of Native American culture (for example, a fry bread study break or a drum group demonstration).

According to former resident fellow David Wellbery, the Native American freshmen, unlike Ujamaa's black residents, do not want to live in Roble, preferring to be treated like all other students on campus. By their second or third year at Stanford, however, they are much more interested in getting back in touch with their Native American heritage by living with other Indians.

A group of Native American students has tried for at least ten years to establish a Native American ethnic theme house on campus. They have expressed dissatisfaction over the fact that the resident fellow at Roble is not an Indian, that their impact in Roble (eight out of 295) is small, and, in particular, that the benefits of a Native American–oriented living situation are not truly available to Native American students.

But the administration has consistently turned down the group's petition for a house. Among the reasons frequently cited for the denial are the small number of Native American undergraduates on campus and their probable inability to support a full-fledged theme house program; the cultural diversity within the Indian community at Stanford (more than forty tribes are represented);

the history of noncooperation and tension among tribes; tensions between reservation and nonreservation Indians; the reluctance of Native American students to identify their ethnicity; tensions between Indians with more or less Indian parentage; and the existence of the Native American Cultural Center.

Although they do not yet have a theme house, Native American students will be moving in the fall of 1985 to newer and smaller quarters in Governor's Corner. There are also signs that the administration is giving more sympathetic attention to their request for a theme house, especially in light of the growing number of Native American students on campus.

It is not surprising that there is controversy today over the mission and goals of the ethnic theme houses and whether or not they represent the best way to foster better racial understanding on campus. They are variously praised by their proponents for offering a minority-dominated environment that exposes minority students, who have spent their whole lives surrounded by white faces and white culture, to their own culture for the first time; for serving as a brake on the co-optation of minority students by the white majority in locating them within their own communities, thus promoting minority identity and sensibility as well as a chance to develop leadership skills; as a place for minority students and the broader minority community to meet; and as a celebration of minority culture that educates both minority and majority students. (How important they are to the non-minority community is a matter of continuous debate.)

While the ethnic theme houses may be offering these and other benefits to their respective constituencies, by all accounts their popularity has waned in recent years. There is evidence that one of the benefits—providing an alternative to living in the white-dominated dorms at Stanford—has become increasingly less important to minority students over the past decade. For example, 53 percent of black freshmen in 1972 expressed a preference for living in Ujamaa, compared to less than half that percentage (22 percent) in 1982. Twenty-nine percent of Asian-American freshmen wanted to live in Okada in 1972; by 1982 it was 15 percent. In 1972, 20 percent of Hispanic freshmen chose to live in Casa Zapata, but by 1982 freshmen interest had dropped to 14 percent.

It is also worth noting that for both blacks and Hispanics, interest in having a co-ethnic roommate also declined—12 percent for black and 18 percent for Hispanic freshmen. Inexplicably, Asian-American freshmen were more interested in rooming with another Asian-American in 1982 (29 percent) than they were in 1972 (25 percent).

Many supporters of the ethnic theme houses feel they are in danger of being dismantled, partly because the University, they charge, has never been fully committed to them. Whether true or false, this suspicion has frequently set the tone of the relationship between the minority community and the administration. Those who defend the houses believe that the University should not have encouraged in the early years the perception that the theme houses were experimental, but should have demonstrated that it was firmly and unambiguously committed to them.

But there are also other problems. One black administrator, for example, has remarked that although Ujamaa has been successful in providing a housing option and a place where black culture can be expressed, it has not been very successful in educating the white community at Stanford. Black students, he said, have developed "a cynical attitude" and have "neglected to reach out to white students." Nor has the University, he adds, done anything to foster positive black-white relations (e.g., no seminars, no dorm meetings about these issues, no sense that these matters are a University priority).

He further notes that Ujamaa residents are often inclined to think of themselves as the "true blacks" at Stanford, labeling those who choose to live elsewhere as the "assimilated" blacks. This, he concedes, is divisive and only adds to Ujamaa's present difficulty in getting students to live there.

While the ethnic theme houses have been trying to encourage cross-cultural learning and the rigorous study of their own respective cultures (some with more purpose and success than others), their most controversial goal has been what Dean James Lyons calls the "enclave" objective—namely, an institutionalized option for a minority to live together in greater "racial" comfort. The University, however, will not permit a theme house to have an "enclave" as its objective, because campus policies prohibit the exclusion of students from any academic program on the basis of race.

The response of many blacks is that the University's opposition to the idea of an ethnic enclave is unwarranted, that blacks could not avoid white society at Stanford or anywhere else in the United States even if they wanted to, and that black students at Stanford are already assimilated, having come typically from suburban areas where they were the only blacks in the neighborhood. In a survey he conducted in May 1982, Assistant Dean of Students Ron Hudson found that 67 percent of black students at Stanford came from white high schools with black populations under 25 percent. "These black students *need* contact with other blacks," Hudson contends. "The novelty is not Stanford, but the theme houses." In other words, being in a predominantly white community is not a new experience, but living primarily with other blacks is.

In 1982, a subcommittee of the Faculty Senate Committee on Undergraduate Studies was charged with reviewing residential education in general. Composed of faculty, administrators, and students, the committee developed the following guidelines for all theme houses:

1) A house must have a well-defined theme.

2) Residential preference should be given to students committed to the theme.

3) Each house should have a group of "keepers of the theme," such as faculty, alumni, and the current resident fellow.

4) The mission of a house cannot be changed without undergoing a review by a University committee. Presumably, this would serve as a check on an ethnic theme house that designed a program emphasizing cross-cultural study and learning but then changed or returned to a racial-comfort theme.

5) A theme house should not be regarded as permanent. The committee called for a full review of a house every three or four years and allowed for the possibility of disbanding the program.

6) Two-thirds to three-fourths of an ethnic theme house should be reserved for ethnic minorities if they want to live in the house. After that, however, every effort should be made to give priority to non-ethnic applicants. The current rule of thumb is one-half minority priority, with the second half available on a first-come, first-served basis independent of ethnicity.

Although few will say so (and then only privately), there appears to be conflict between the administration and the black and Chicano communities on campus over the conduct and goals of Ujamaa and Casa Zapata. The administration is interested primarily in having the houses present all Stanford students with an opportunity to experience an American ethnic program that has substantial academic merit, advances minority–non-minority cooperation, and promotes intergroup harmony and learning. A very secondary goal is to address the issue of making minority students more racially comfortable, and this as unobtrusively as possible.

These divergent perspectives reflect much of the current debate over the future direction of race relations in the United States. What it suggests about the ethnic theme houses at Stanford is unclear. Both their supporters and detractors would agree that the houses do tend to separate minority from majority students. But they do not agree on whether this promotes an undesirable or unhealthy segregation on campus.

To date, the University has played a small role in shaping the goals of the theme houses. Although each house completes a self-evaluation each year, Dean Lyons has said that it has been extremely difficult for his office to conduct an inquiry into their organization and performance. The minority communities on campus tend to regard such questioning as further indication that the University remains uncertain and ambiguous about its commitment to the ethnic theme houses.

This is one of several issues creating what has been described as a "fundamental tension" between administrators and the ethnic theme houses—"terribly sensitive issues that have a high potential for political combustion," as one faculty observer put it. The University generally has looked upon the houses as successful, he acknowledges, "but it has also pretty much left them alone." The question now is whether it will become more directly involved in monitoring and guiding their activities. If so, the decision is not likely to be without cost.

The ethnic theme houses at Stanford have generated debate and controversy on the campus ever since they began operation in the early 1970s. It was not surprising, therefore, that more than a year ago a Faculty Senate Committee was charged with reviewing the residential education program in general and the theme houses in particular. Yet little of a systematic nature has been known and made public about how students view the ethnic theme houses. What kinds of experiences have they had with them? What do they see as the houses' goals? Do they believe the theme houses promote good relations between minority and non-minority students, or do they perceive them as divisive?

In the spring quarter of 1984 I, along with my research assistant, Jeanne Fleming, conducted a student survey in which we sought to describe and analyze students' familiarity with the ethnic theme houses, the level of student support for them, and how student attitudes toward the houses vary among different groups on campus. In early April 1984, questionnaires were mailed out to a 50 percent sample of seniors listed in the 1984 *Stanford Student Directory*, 806 names selected using a random number generating process. Seniors were singled out because we wanted to be certain that our respondents would have had ample time to become acquainted with the theme houses. The return rate was 54 percent.

In addition, in-depth interviews with 30 students (from freshmen to graduate) were conducted by two undergraduates, one black and one white. Of those interviewed, 23 had at some point lived in either Okada (the Asian-American theme house), Ujamaa (the black theme house), or Zapata (the Chicano theme house) and were able to provide a wide range of personal comments and insights.

Although most of the seniors who responded to the survey had a passing acquaintance with the ethnic theme houses, few had spent much time in them or participated in theme house activities. Forty-five percent of blacks and 17 percent of Chicanos, but only 11 percent of whites and 8 percent of Asian-Americans, reported spending time in the theme houses or knowing "a lot" about them. While no point of comparison with any other residential education program is possible, these figures indicate that the level of student involvement with the theme houses is low.

The seniors were asked how important they felt it was for the theme houses to 1) provide a place for minority students to get away from the dominant, non-minority culture on campus, 2) foster better relations between ethnic groups, 3) encourage minority students to develop and keep their cultural identities, 4) promote serious study of minority culture, and 5) expose non-minority students to minority cultures. Substantial majorities agreed that almost all of these goals were "important" or "somewhat important," with percentages ranging from 79 percent to 83 percent. A notable exception was the "minority refuge" goals. Only 41 percent said it was "important" or "somewhat important" for the theme houses to provide a place for minority students to get away from non-minority Stanford.

The percentage of those who said the "minority refuge" or (as some University officials often refer to it) "ethnic enclave" goal is important varied considerably, however, depending on the person's political views. Forty-nine percent of those who called themselves "very liberal" said the "minority refuge" goal is "important" or "very important," compared to 24 percent who identified themselves as "very conservative."

Ethnicity is also related to student opinion on this particular goal, with whites less in favor of the "minority refuge" concept than either blacks or Chicanos, but more approving than Asian-Americans. Thus, the ethnic theme houses' aim of providing a place for minorities to get away from white Stanford would seem to be more crucial, and presumably more salient, for minority groups themselves (with the possible exception of Asian-Americans) than for whites. (As was noted earlier, it is this aspect of the theme houses that has been troublesome to Stanford's administration, and perhaps at the same time most cherished by theme house supporters.)

When asked how well the theme houses are *meeting* each of the five goals, the students' evaluations were very different from their assessment of the *importance* of each goal. Sixty percent of all respondents said the theme houses are doing an "excellent" or "good" job in providing a minority refuge, and 55 percent gave the same response in appraising the success of the houses in helping minority students retain their cultural identities. But no more than 8 percent thought the houses are doing an "excellent" or "good" job of fostering better relations between minority and non-minority groups on campus. Furthermore, only 22 percent gave similar ratings for exposing non-minorities to minority cultures, and 31 percent for promoting the serious study of minority cultures.

But, once again, ethnicity plays an important part in the graduating seniors' evaluation of the success of the ethnic theme houses in achieving the five goals. For example, 75 percent of blacks

Student Ethnic Groups at Stanford

	DIRECTORY	PERCENT	SURVEY	PERCENT
Asian	139	8.32	37	8.8
Black	88	5.26	16	3.8
Chicano	95	5.68	18*	4.3*
Other Hispanic	8	.47	—	—
Native American	6	.40	3	.7
Foreign	63	3.77	—	—
White	1,267	75.82	335	79.6
Other	—	—	8	1.9
Missing Data	—	—	4	1.0

* Includes other Hispanics

The chart above shows the proportion of students in each ethnic group listed in the student directory in 1984, according to the Stanford Registrar's Office, compared to the proportion of students in each ethnic group in the Stanford Student Survey.

As can be seen, the survey had a smaller percentage of blacks and Chicanos, and a larger percentage of Asians and Native Americans, than did the population of Stanford seniors as a whole. The survey also had a slightly higher ratio of women to men than did the senior population.

and 72 percent of Chicanos said the houses are doing an "excellent" or "good" job in achieving the "minority refuge" goal, compared to 61 percent of whites. Asian-American respondents were less positive, with only 46 percent answering "excellent" or "good." When asked about the goal of helping minority students maintain their cultural identities, the percentages saying "excellent" or "good" were 81 percent (blacks), 88 percent (Chicanos), 56 percent (Asian-Americans), and 52 percent (whites). And although no ethnic group strongly believes that the theme houses are doing a very good job of fostering better relations between different groups, minorities are considerably more likely than whites to think they do.

In short, Stanford seniors feel the ethnic theme houses are doing a much better job of serving the internal needs of their respective ethnic communities than of addressing the relationship between minority and non-minority students—and this in the face of the students' strongly shared view that the houses should be emphasizing the latter at least as much as the former.

In responding to a series of questions about their own *personal* experiences with the ethnic theme houses, seniors were essentially split on whether they felt welcome (42 percent) or not (43 percent) at the houses. Twenty-eight percent said their contact with the houses had given them a chance to get to know minority students, but 58 percent disagreed. Not surprisingly, minority students, especially blacks, were much more likely than non-minority students to say they felt welcome at the theme houses. And while substantial percentages of minorities thought that the ethnic theme houses helped them to get to know other minority students, only 25 percent of white students agreed. Again, a consistent pattern emerges: Minority students approve of and feel much more comfortable in the ethnic theme houses than do non-minorities.

Political views also shaped opinion on these two questions. Stanford seniors who said they were "very liberal" (49 percent) were more likely to say they felt welcome at the theme houses than were those who said they were "very conservative" (19 percent). The same pattern held true for those who felt that the theme houses make it easier to meet minority students, with 36 percent of "very liberal" students but only 21 percent of "very conservative" students agreeing.

Two questions were asked in an effort to determine if students believe that the ethnic theme houses are bringing about better ethnic relations on campus. This is the heart of the controversy over whether the houses should be primarily oriented to their own minority needs or to serving the broader Stanford community by encouraging intergroup harmony. Sixteen percent said they thought the theme houses encourage minority and non-minority students to get to know each other, but 50 percent said the houses discourage interracial friendship. Twenty-six percent thought they did neither. When asked if they thought that the theme houses *promoted* separatism, integration, or neither, almost three-quarters of the students said the houses promote separatism. Their responses leave little doubt that students are much more likely to regard the theme houses as a force against interaction and friendship among minorities and non-minorities.

Again, minorities and non-minorities gave different answers to these two questions. Thirty-one percent of blacks, 32 percent of Asian-Americans, and 22 percent of Chicanos said they felt the ethnic theme houses encourage minority/non-minority friendships, compared to 13 percent of whites. Even more dramatic, 54 percent of whites said the houses discourage such friendships, while only 28 percent of Chicanos, 27 percent of Asian-Americans, and 19 percent of blacks agreed with their sentiments. Regardless of ethnicity, few would say that the theme houses advance the cause of integration, and substantial percentages of all four groups feel that the forces of separatism are pronounced.

Further evidence of this generally negative view of the houses' role in fostering integration and interethnic harmony can be seen in the way students assess the state of affairs between minority and non-minority residents in the theme houses, that is, blacks and whites living in Ujamaa, Chicanos and whites in Casa Zapata, and Asian-Americans and whites in Okada. Nine percent said the relationship is "excellent" or "good" in Ujamaa and in Casa Zapata, and 35 percent felt that way about Okada. The percentages reporting the relationship as "fair" or "poor" were nearly the reverse: 31 percent, 33 percent, and 9 percent respectively. Although there is a marked difference in attitude toward the theme houses—with evaluation of Okada much more favorable than of the other two houses—opinion about how students of different ethnic backgrounds are getting along in Ujamaa and Casa Zapata is not encouraging.

This assessment is in sharp contrast to the way students view the relationship between ethnic groups in their own residences specifically and at Stanford generally. For example, 50 percent of the seniors characterized the relationship between blacks and whites in their own living quarters as "excellent" or "good," with 48 percent giving the same answer for Chicanos and whites and 55 percent for Asian-Americans and whites. As for the relationship between these groups on the campus as a whole, 57 percent, 53 percent, and 83 percent, respectively, said it was "excellent" or "good."

Although the majority of students see the ethnic theme houses as basically separatist, they believe they still have a place on campus. Only 20 percent favored abolishing them. Fifty-seven percent thought that Stanford should continue to support them, but that some changes need to be made. Blacks and Asian-Americans were much more likely than whites to say that the houses should continue just as they are. However, most members of each ethnic group (56 percent of blacks, 67 percent of Chicanos, 49 percent of Asian-Americans, 57 percent of whites) favored changes in the houses.

(Given the choice of supporting the ethnic theme houses as they are, abolishing them, or supporting them with changes, it is perhaps not surprising that a majority favored the latter option. In the spring of 1985, Stanford's Office of Residential Education sponsored a survey of students to assess the "quality of life" in campus residences. The results should provide a useful context in which to evaluate further some of the findings about students' reactions to the ethnic theme houses presented here.)

Of the in-depth interviews with students who had lived in an ethnic theme house, fourteen were with blacks, twelve with whites, three with Mexican-Americans, and one with an Asian-American. All of the black students were interviewed by a black undergraduate, and virtually all of the white students were interviewed by a white undergraduate.

As borne out by the survey, the black students liked the theme houses and felt they are needed at Stanford. "I like the fact that I can go to my house and see my friends who are of the same ethnic background," said a black woman. "The ethnic theme house puts back that part of my life that I am used to," another black woman said. "Stanford is a totally different way of life, with many students whose parents have money and thus so do their kids. I am not used to this way of life," she added, "and neither are most other minorities."

A black woman senior put some of her feelings very simply: "I like not having to explain to people in the house how I wash and press my hair. I just basically feel more comfortable living with people of the same cultural background." Other blacks talked of the type of security Ujamaa provides and of the warmth and friendliness from students like themselves who have similar interests and ideas. "Without the house," one of them said, "this feeling would turn into curiosity, fear, and other types of stress."

But black student opinion is not monolithic. While all of those interviewed endorsed the general purposes of the theme houses, some found fault with the way they are run. Others thought the houses should do more to foster integrated activities—in the words of one black senior, "This should be one of their goals if it isn't already. Too many times I see parties in Ujamaa where 99 percent are black students." Several black students stressed that a primary goal should be to promote cultural diversity. "I would think that would be how Residential Education and the institution of Stanford would interpret the purpose of the theme houses," a black graduate student said. "I think the goals are fine, but I don't see many results."

The white students were more critical of the theme houses, especially of their experiences in Ujamaa and Zapata. "When I lived in Zapata, there were no pluses," said a senior. "It shouldn't be a center for far-left politics and nothing else. I was not able to express my opinions without being labeled racist, sexist, or an idiot. Many people were labeled something before they even got there."

A white senior who lived for a semester in Ujamaa said he did not benefit much from the experience "because I didn't want to be there. The blacks thought it was their house. This created controversy. At times it was tense. It ended up being segregated." One white student who had lived in both Ujamaa and Okada said he really enjoyed Okada, especially the exposure to people from different countries and backgrounds. In Ujamaa, he said, there were too many people "who weren't reaching out. I felt left out. I would recommend living in Okada but I would not recommend Ujamaa to anyone."

Other white students also liked Okada. A junior who had lived in Branner and Burbank characterized Okada as "more friendly, less violent, less rowdy. It's easier to sleep here and I meet friendlier people." Another white student said, "I hate to stereotype Asians, but stereo-blasting is not commonplace here. It's quiet and peaceful. I like Stanford dorms in general," he added, "and this is really just a Stanford dorm with minor variations."

In these extended interviews (some lasted more than two hours), all 30 students were asked to comment on perhaps the most important and (for many observers) troubling question of all—how well integrated they felt the minority and non-minority students were in the ethnic theme houses. Do they pretty much keep to themselves? Do they eat together? Do they have parties together? Do they develop close friendships? Do the ethnic theme houses have any effect on interracial dating? Some of their answers, wide-ranging and diverse, are worth reporting verbatim.

> I would say that the house is well integrated, but most ethnic groups tend to keep to themselves and deal with members only of their ethnic background. But that is the way of the world which I believe Stanford cannot cure. . . . Most people tend to have friends who are of the same background and have similar tastes, which may be the reason for the in-house segregation. . . . Mostly minority students would be interested in the house because it is centered around the ethnic groups and their culture. . . . More interracial relationships happen outside the house because most people outside of the house are non-minorities. . . . I have not ever dated a non-minority member, but for students generally it is discouraged, especially in Ujamaa. The minorities feel that if you have a white boyfriend or girlfriend, then you are not considered one of the ethnic minority even if your skin is darker than night.
>
> *Black sophomore woman*

> You learn about another culture. You have to interact with people who are radically different. It's uncomfortable, but you learn. . . . It was trying, but worthwhile. I can't compare any year with the one in Zapata. . . . What I liked least was the separatism. It was strange to deal with. I had never met two groups that were antagonistic like that. . . . As a minority in the dorm I was expected to choose [the right friends] and take part in the

separatism. I couldn't understand that. One person came up to me and said, 'Why don't you stick to your own?' Before, we never looked at ourselves as Chicanos. We were Mexican-Americans. . . . It was hard to come into the University and have to say what you are. . . . It was not well integrated. . . . Within the house segregation is fostered. . . . I wish they could do away with the theme houses. The bad outweighs the good. The segregation outweighs the positive aspects.

Mexican-American senior man

Living in Okada for three years has had a definite effect on me. I've become more social. . . . We orient the dorm as a place to live rather than a theme house. . . . You always have a few little cliques, but even they're mixed. It's very well integrated. Don't think of people as Asians or non-Asians. No divisions. Don't look for it and don't see it. We get people together with the same interests, but not by race.

Mexican-American senior man

I don't have to put up with any subtle racial slurs when living in Ujamaa. Students there understand why I behave a certain way. . . . The theme houses are integrated because the house is still 50 percent minority. Just because black students don't sit and converse with white students because they are off talking to other minority students does not necessarily mean that this is an act of segregation. . . . I would call it a more preferred type of segregation where students sit and talk and eat together because those people are considered friends. . . . Inside the house there is more discouragement to willfully go about seeking white friends—black students will refuse to acknowledge you and will not confide in you as much. Interracial dating is looked down upon. . . .

Black senior man

It is a plus for Stanford at least to say they have [ethnic theme houses]. It gives [minorities] a place. Gives them orientation. Externally it looks good, but internally they don't work. People who haven't lived there don't know what they are. They just know they don't want to live there. . . . [The theme houses] encourage segregation. People want their own house apart from others. . . . I had minority roomates each year. The one I am least friendly with now was one from Ujamaa. It hurts relationships because you are conscious of color. . . .

White senior man

I am more likely to sit with another black person at dinner than a white person, but I don't know why. . . . I think that the blacks and whites prefer to be with each other. If someone were to ask me, 'Why are you sitting with all those black people?', I would say, 'Because they are my friends.'. . . Students living in [Ujamaa] must come in contact with each other so it forces integration. . . . Interracial dating would have to be extremely underground because the house discourages it. Theme houses have a negative effect on interracial dating because the peer pressure would be too great against having a white boyfriend or girlfriend. Once I had a white male friend come over to the theme house and I was talking with other minorities of the house who, when they saw him, decided to leave because they don't approve.

Black senior woman

Overall, living in the theme house has been a good experience for me. What I like most is that I feel comfortable. . . . For those who live in the house it is a great experience, but for those who don't, the theme house does not play a great role, and that's the problem. . . . I think the negative perceptions [of the theme houses] are based on ignorance, and those who do not live there are usually ignorant. . . . To tell you the truth, I think [the theme houses] foster segregation. . . . It is a very difficult subject to deal with in society at large. How do you deal with the problem? Stanford's theme houses cannot solve what problems there are in society. Then you have white liberals who try to believe that everything is equal, but they are naive to believe that Stanford has now solved the problem with ethnic theme houses.

Black senior woman

During the past twenty years, Stanford has accepted a growing number of blacks, Mexican-Americans, and other minorities. It represents a fundamental change for the campus, a change that tends to anchor the University's consciousness of its image in the larger and more diverse society it aspires to reflect. The days of "the Farm"—virtually all-white, almost pastoral in its peace and charm, and quietly set apart from the currents and conflicts of the rest of the world—are gone. Having demonstrated its determination and capacity to admit many more students from various groups and backgrounds, Stanford now faces the challenge of whether and how it can help forge closer relationships, if not binding ties, among them.

There is no evidence to suggest that the University administration wishes to discontinue the ethnic theme houses as a residential option on campus. There is evidence to suggest that there might be room for some changes in the theme houses' organization, mission, and goals. How can more tolerance and understanding be fostered in the ethnic theme houses? Some of the problems that this survey of student opinion has underlined—in particular, the perceived separatist climate and tendencies in some of the theme houses—are not likely to be resolved unless the University assumes a more active role.

Stanford has committed itself to more minority-group representation on campus because (among other reasons) it firmly believes that an ethnically diverse student body will enable students of different races to benefit from a chance to study and learn together. But how much diversity is desirable? In the midst of diversity, are there times when homogeneity may be preferable? If diversity is educationally important in the classroom, is it equally important across the entire University, and to what degree?

As we have seen, many minority students support the ethnic theme houses because they want to live together in greater "racial" comfort and away from white Stanford. In their view this is one of the benefits of homogeneity. But does this mean that an increasingly diverse student body should be permitted or encouraged by the University to "self-select" into tight and separatist homogeneous living groups? And, if so, would some of the objectives of educational diversity at Stanford be compromised?

The Portable Stanford Book Series

This is a volume of the Portable Stanford Book Series, published by the Stanford Alumni Association. Subscribers receive each new Portable Stanford volume on approval. The following books may also be ordered, by number, on the adjoining card:

$12.95 titles

- *Race Relations on Campus: Stanford Students Speak* by John H. Bunzel (#4062)
- *The Sleepwatchers* by William C. Dement (#4059)
- *Around California in 1891* by Terence Emmons (#4060)
- *Technology and Culture: A Historical Romance* by Barry M. Katz (#4057)
- *2020 Visions: Long View of a Changing World* by Richard Carlson and Bruce Goldman (#4055)
- *"What Is to Be Done?" Soviets at the Edge* by John G. Gurley (#4056)
- *Brief Lessons in High Technology: A Primer on Seven Fields that Are Changing Our Lives* edited by James Meindl (#4045)
- *Terra Non Firma: Understanding and Preparing for Earthquakes* by James M. Gere and Haresh C. Shah (#4030)

$10.95 titles

- *Notable or Notorious? A Gallery of Parisians* by Gordon Wright (#4052)
- *This Boy's Life* by Tobias Wolff (#4050)
- *Ride the Tiger to the Mountain: T'ai Chi for Health* by Martin and Emily Lee and JoAn Johnstone (#4047)
- *Alpha and Omega: Ethics at the Frontiers of Life and Death* by Ernlé W.D. Young (#4046)
- *Conceptual Blockbusting* (third edition) by James L. Adams (#4007)
- *In My Father's House: Tales of an Unconformable Man* by Nancy Huddleston Packer (#4040)
- *The Imperfect Art: Reflections on Jazz and Modern Culture* by Ted Gioia (#4048)
- *Yangtze: Nature, History, and the River* by Lyman P. Van Slyke (#4043)
- *The Eagle and the Rising Sun: America and Japan in the Twentieth Century* by John K. Emmerson and Harrison M. Holland (#4044)
- *The Care and Feeding of Ideas* by James L. Adams (#4042)
- *The American Way of Life Need Not Be Hazardous to Your Health* (revised edition) by John W. Farquhar, M.D. (#4018)
- *Cory Aquino and the People of the Philippines* by Claude A. Buss (#4041)
- *Under the Gun: Nuclear Weapons and the Superpowers* by Coit D. Blacker (#4039)
- *50: Midlife in Perspective* by Herant Katchadourian, M.D. (#4038)

- *Wide Awake at 3:00 A.M.: By Choice or By Chance?* by Richard M. Coleman (#4036)
- *Hormones: The Messengers of Life* by Lawrence Crapo, M.D. (#4035)
- *Panic: Facing Fears, Phobias, and Anxiety* by Stewart Agras, M.D. (#4034)
- *Who Controls Our Schools? American Values in Conflict* by Michael W. Kirst (#4033)
- *Matters of Life and Death: Risks vs. Benefits of Medical Care* by Eugene D. Robin, M.D. (#4032)
- *On Nineteen Eighty-Four* edited by Peter Stansky (#4031)
- *The Musical Experience: Sound, Movement, and Arrival* by Leonard G. Ratner (#4029)
- *Challenges to Communism* by John G. Gurley (#4028)
- *Cosmic Horizons: Understanding the Universe* by Robert V. Wagoner and Donald W. Goldsmith (#4027)
- *Beyond the Turning Point: The U.S. Economy in the 1980s* by Ezra Solomon (#4026)
- *The Age of Television* by Martin Esslin (#4025)
- *Insiders and Outliers: A Procession of Frenchmen* by Gordon Wright (#4024)
- *Mirror and Mirage: Fiction by Nineteen* by Albert J. Guerard (#4023)
- *The Touch of Time: Myth, Memory, and the Self* by Albert J. Guerard (#4022)
- *The Politics of Contraception* by Carl Djerassi (#4020)
- *Economic Policy Beyond the Headlines* by George P. Shultz and Kenneth W. Dam (#4017)
- *Tales of an Old Ocean* by Tjeerd van Andel (#4016)
- *Law Without Lawyers: A Comparative View of Law in China and the United States* by Victor H. Li (#4015)
- *The World That Could Be* by Robert C. North (#4014)
- *America: The View from Europe* by J. Martin Evans (#4013)
- *An Incomplete Guide to the Future* by Willis W. Harman (#4012)
- *Murder and Madness* by Donald T. Lunde, M.D. (#4010)
- *The Anxious Economy* by Ezra Solomon (#4009)
- *The Galactic Club: Intelligent Life in Outer Space* by Ronald Bracewell (#4008)
- *Is Man Incomprehensible to Man?* by Philip H. Rhinelander (#4005)
- *Some Must Watch While Some Must Sleep* by William E. Dement, M.D. (#4003)
- *Human Sexuality: Sense and Nonsense* by Herant Katchadourian, M.D. (#4002)